IF I COULD ONLY BE SURE: THE LIFE OF NOLAN PORTER

PATRICE "CANDY" ZAPPA

CREDITS

"If I Could Only Be Sure: The Life Of Nolan Porter" was completed on November 26, 2021.

All photos are from the collections of Nolan Porter and Patrice "Candy" Zappa unless otherwise noted.

Layout and design by Greg Russo. Front cover photo/effects (from the Messaround at Viva Cantina, Burbank, California on February 16, 2014) by Spencer Filichia. Many thanks to Spencer for his permission to use this excellent photo.

First edition - November 2021.

Copyright © 2021 by Patrice "Candy" Zappa.

All rights reserved, including the right of reproduction in whole or in part in any form.

Special thanks: Greg Russo, Julie Waterman, Larry Rogak, Mari Linville, Stone Foundation, The Signatures, Mark Wheaton, Nolan Porter's fans worldwide, plus all the people that contributed their recollections.

Crossfire Publications, 54 Chester Avenue, Stewart Manor, NY 11530.

email: crossfirepublications@gmail.com

Patrice Zappa maintains Nolan Porter's page on Facebook:
https://www.facebook.com/nolan.f.porter

ISBN-13: 978-0-9983550-6-1

To subscribe to the Nolan Porter mailing list with access to exclusive recordings, please send your email to crossfirepublications@gmail.com.

TABLE OF CONTENTS

Introduction (by Greg Russo)	4
The Ending/ Our Beginning	5
Where It All Started	52
Behind the Scenes	77
Friends and Family Remember Nolan Porter	82
Nolan Porter Discography:	
› Singles	116
› Albums	117
› Sessionography for the Lizard, Vulture and ABC Labels	119
› Unreleased Tracks	121
› Videos	121
› BBC Music Sessions with Stone Foundation	121
› Television - Career Highlights	121
Related Books and Music	122

INTRODUCTION

Nolan Porter was an absolutely brilliant man in so many ways. Not only was Nolan a man of numerous talents, he was able to positively touch a diverse collection of people. Music fans of course are very familiar with Nolan Porter's records and/or stage performances, but very few people know that he was a fixture at Westside Regional Center in Culver City, California. In addition to brightening the lives of people with developmental disabilities, Nolan's work associates at Westside were very aware of how well he enriched their lives to the point that they performed their roles at a much higher level than they thought possible. Testimonials from fellow workers, musical acquaintances and personal friends prove that point extremely well. Each recollection reveals the immensity of this man Nolan Porter. You will be amazed and astounded by what Nolan accomplished here on earth.

The initial recordings that Nolan made in the early 1970s were made with former members of Frank Zappa's Mothers Of Invention, but it was not until other musicians entered the picture that Nolan Porter found his own musical voice. Northern Soul classics such as "Keep On Keeping On," "If I Could Only Be Sure" and "Oh Baby" were created as Nolan relied on his own soul and R&B instincts. While these songs and many others are considered highly today, the original record releases were designed to marginalize Nolan's talents, his name, and more importantly, his income. A lesser man would be crushed by such poor record company treatment over a lifetime, but Nolan rose above it all to lift the spirits of his audiences for the 50 years that followed his first recorded works.

After meeting Patrice "Candy" Zappa in 2001, I met Nolan Porter in person three years later when I was recording my "Neonfire" album. When I visited Nolan and Candy in California, I was amazed by what they did to elevate the vocals and melodies of my songs. Nolan knew immediately what songs he or Candy could do lead on and what songs they could do together. Nolan had a wealth of different ideas upon which to draw. We all ended up being very happy with the final results. The Nolan/Candy pairing was a personal and musical match made in heaven.

We all wish that we had a Nolan Porter in our lives. Nolan could naturally take in the ambience of a place and make the best outcome for everyone around him. You knew that you were in the presence of someone really special.

Nolan never thought highly of himself to start working on an autobiography. He was more focused on others. After a lot of arm-twisting, Nolan finally agreed that he should start assembling materials for such a career work. Unfortunately, as soon as things were to get underway, Nolan became seriously ill. This book is the closest we will ever come to what Nolan would have produced on his own, and it is very close indeed.

I am very blessed to have known Nolan Porter - the Westside employee, the musician, the legend, and the finest example of a man that made everyone else feel worthwhile and loved.

GREG RUSSO
Author of "Cosmik Debris: The Collected History & Improvisations Of Frank Zappa"
October 22, 2021

THE ENDING

February 4, 2021

I looked in his eyes and held my hand on his chest. I could feel his pulse, thready and weak. I told him he was the best man I ever had and that I loved him with all my heart. I told him that I would be okay and to let go. With that, he quietly and gently passed away. That was the last time I felt the life of Nolan Porter. My life would forever change after that moment.

OUR BEGINNING

Back in 1999, I was at a karaoke contest at a place called Leon's Steakhouse, in North Hollywood, California. I was asked to judge the contest. A very lovely woman approached me. We struck up a conversation and hit it off immediately. The woman I met, Mari Linville, told me about a friend of hers, Nolan Porter. She told me that he was a singer and that I really should meet him. As time went by, she also told Nolan about me and we would talk over the phone, but we hadn't met in person yet. This was not fast enough for Mari, so she decided to take matters into her own hands. The day after Nolan's 50th birthday, she invited him to Leon's and likewise invited me for the same night. As I walked into Leon's and arrived at Mari's table, I saw Nolan sitting there. As he turned to look at me, he smiled and it looked like he was already sprung. He must have liked what he saw, but I wasn't so sure. I mean really, how can I sit there with Mari and have girl talk with a guy sitting there? I wasn't as pleasant as I usually am, but as the evening wore on, I mellowed out. We both got up to sing "Too Much, Too Little, Too Late" by Johnny Mathis and Deniece Williams.

We looked at each other with a look of surprise as we realized how good we sounded together! We had subsequent meetings at our place, as it later became, and sang several songs together at karaoke.

Our voices blended so well that we decided to put something together. We scoured the Valley and Los Angeles area for venues to perform at. That effort took longer than we realized, so we decided to put our own show together. We worked tirelessly. Nolan was like a Trojan, arranging and producing a fabulous show in 2000 that we called "Once A Legacy." We managed to get a spot at the Simi Valley Cultural Center. He hired terrific musicians, and I had a photographic montage on screen of my family along with music and skits. We performed music from the '60s and '70s. It was a night full of memories.

> Patrice Zappa
>
> Nolan Porter
>
> 2 Unique Voices
>
> That Blend Into One

Two days later, Nolan was getting up to go to work. He was exhausted and I told him to stay home. Being a stubborn Taurus, he said he was fine and went to work. Later, he told me that after fellow workers were congratulating him on a super show, he went to the men's room and proceeded to vomit profusely. He was so sick. He left work to come home, only he didn't make it. In fact, he never made it to his car. He passed out in the park near his work and laid on the ground for four hours. When he finally got to his car, he drove to my mom's house. I was at work, and mom called to tell me that Nolan was lying on her living room floor. I went there after work and brought him back to my place. As I was telling

Nolan and I at the first "Once A Legacy" show on November 12, 2000.

him, in my own inimitable way, "I told you so," he agreed that he should have listened to me and stayed home.

Stress is a killer, and coupled with his penchant of staying up late, getting up early to be at work, lots of coffee and then putting in hours of rehearsal for the show finally took its toll on him. I believe it finally took its toll on his life.

Working on that show opened my eyes to a lot of things about Nolan. He was a stickler for making things work out just right. He was accommodating to me and the other musicians, and that attitude followed us for the rest of our musical lives. Nolan was a pro, and we were our biggest fans of each other. We made sure the musicians, and they were excellent musicians, were paid and fed while Nolan and I seldom received any monetary compensation. Our rehearsals were usually 3-5 hours, but we took care of everyone.

Nolan and his mom Estell.

Nolan was born and raised in Los Angeles, California. His parents divorced when he was very young. The absence of his father in the home made a lasting impression on him, whether he knew it or not. Nolan was a curious, noisy boy as most boys are. But when the noise got too much for his mother, she would send him away, to either live with friends or to boarding schools. Nolan, being the friendly and sometimes guileless young boy that he was (and that carried over into his adult years at times) made friends easily and was well liked. He didn't know anything about prejudice or bigotry, even when some dullard called him a derogatory name. Nolan went home and asked his mother what it meant. He was close to his father, but Nolan told me that when his father was younger, he was angry all the time. Sometimes, Nolan got angry too, in his youth, but later on it was rare. Nolan was briefly married to a woman named Sharon during his early recording career, but that did not work out. He was related to, by marriage, Charlie Mingus and somewhere down the line at the 4th ward in Texas, Joe Sample.

Nolan was loyal. His friends meant the world to him, and he had friends from 40-50 years before. Nolan didn't have any biological children of his own, but he had a godson, Aidan, he was a stepdad to my kids and family, and kids of friends' kids meant the world to him as well. He was always remembering the birthdays of his nieces and nephews. Many times, he would ask me to help pick out a present for them. Instead of racking our brains for the perfect gift, the one thing that never doesn't fit, money is the perfect color and you never need to exchange it! I'd tell him to just get a nice card and slip in some money, and they will be able to buy whatever they want! It was always a crowd pleaser, and his family loved him.

Nolan loved his freedom and fought hard for it. Early on in our relationship, he wasn't ready, or so he said, for a relationship, and particularly not one with another singer. I could see the attraction between us there, but I didn't want to get involved with him if he always had his hand on the doorknob. It was something I had said to him a couple of times. He was content with just being friends, and he told me that one night as we were leaving our

favorite place to go to our respective homes. As he got near his car, I yelled to him, "I don't fuck my friends." He stopped with a shocked look on his face, because I guess at that time, he did. Friendship was very important to him, and if there's a little icing on the pie, well, so much the better. He acted like he didn't want any kind of reference to each other as boyfriend or girlfriend. One day, while talking to him on the phone, he referred to himself as my boyfriend, and I stopped and asked him to repeat that. And he did. I was getting closer. If it looked like I was upset or ignoring him, he would come back with a big gesture.

When Nolan and I first met, he was a self-assured, independent man. At least, that's how he seemed to me. As years went by, he sometimes seemed a little more dependent on me and that was all right. We sort of leaned on each other at times.

He had been in a boarding school and was a vegetarian, so meat wasn't high on his list of food. While at work one day, the phone rang and as I answered it. Instead of "Hi, how are you?" it was "What do you want, steak or chicken?" I said, "Steak, of course." So, I was treated to a steak dinner that night. I was getting closer.

On one of our first dinner dates, he took me to one of his favorite Japanese restaurants called Kouraku in downtown Los Angeles. Nolan loved Asian food like I love chocolate! The cooks and waitresses all knew him and thought he was too skinny, so they heaped on the rice. Little did they know, it wasn't good for his diabetes, which reared its ugly head before that. I discovered mabo ramen, and that was my favorite dish whenever we went there.

At the end of 1999, we sang at a New Year's Eve party at the Simi Valley Cultural Arts Center after a play. On the way over there, Nolan made it clear that at midnight there would be no tonsil hockey going on. Yeah, OK. So, when the ball went down and everyone yelled "Happy New Year," he grabbed me and gave the kiss that said, "OK, I'm in." I was getting closer.

We refined our "Once A Legacy" show after its first performance. Following work or on weekends, we continued making it even better. It was a real labor of love. Nolan put all of himself into it, as did I. Nolan's friend Irene Silbert did the lighting for us, and my friend Vicki Mahoney helped me change costumes. It was quite a presentation! That was the real start of our musical relationship for the next 22 years.

In 2000, our first getaway trip was to Ventura, and it was our first Valentine's Day together. To surprise him, I had a bouquet of red roses (his favorite) delivered to the room before we got there. When we got in the room and he saw them he said, "Oh, how lovely...I wonder who sent them?" I said, "I did, who else would send roses to you on Valentine's Day?" He smirked. I was getting closer. Wasn't I?

We had a great time, and I was really getting to know him on a more personal basis. It seems that the friendship coupled with a little extra stuff was good. On Monday, I came home from work, opened the front and back doors, as it was warm, and was just about to sit down at my computer when I heard a lovely "Hello" and Nolan showed up with a small potted baby rose plant. I was getting closer.

I introduced Nolan to my mom one day. When they met, he said, "It's nice to meet you, Mrs. Zappa." Mom came back with: "My name is Rose Marie!" I said, "That's it, you're in!" They had a really close relationship, and Nolan was always there for me, especially when it came time for me to be a caregiver for mom. Since we lived on the same street, I was at mom's all the time.

In May of 2000, Nolan and I went up to Ventura to have him meet my two daughters, Julie and Eva. There was instant rapport all around, and I was very happy about that. Later that evening, we came home. As I was lying on my bed, Nolan sat on the side of my bed and held my hand. He told me that, again, he wasn't ready for a relationship, but we could still work on music and only music. After the steam cleared from my ears, I told him that if that's how he wanted it, he wasn't going to like me very much.

It's the whole package with me. I said, "I'm not very nice when it comes to just working on music." Of course, that isn't true – I just get testy. Anyway, he left and it was touch and go for a while, and my closer thing was not so close. I was very upset with the situation, so I decided to look elsewhere for partnership and almost had someone too. Nolan must have sniffed something in the air. Remember that phone call about the steak or chicken inquiry? Well, that was it. He came over a few nights later and brought a movie and dinner. After dinner, I laid down on the floor with a pillow to watch the movie "What Dreams May Come." He sat on the sofa. Within a couple of minutes, he put a pillow up against mine and laid on the floor too - and proceeded to fall asleep. Was I getting closer?

As 2001 started, I was taken in for hysterectomy. It was at that time I really found out how Nolan felt about me and I for him. In the prep room, after they gave me the "happy shot," we overheard two people standing outside the curtain whispering about who I was. I looked at Nolan and said: "Here we go...". They were just about to take me to the operating room when I turned to Nolan and said, "I'd really love to be married to you." (It might have been the result of the happy shot!) His eyes widened and he looked like a frightened horse. He said, "Oh, I don't think I'd make a good husband. I make a better boyfriend." I said, "You suck as a boyfriend. You'd make a better husband." That horse went from frightened to terrified!

Needless to say, the operation was a success and I was glad it was over. Let the mustache and baritone voice begin! I was put gently into my hospital bed, and as that was going on, the nurse and Nolan were there to help. Another nurse informed me that her nephew played bass. You can guess where that was going. I told her to give the info to Nolan. I just wanted to go to sleep. Five days and lots of Vicodin later, I was released. I had given my apartment key to my mom, so my friend Shirley picked me up and took me to my mom's place. It was a duplex that Frank bought for my parents years before, and a few celebrities like Steve Vai and Hugh Masekela occupied the other half of it. This time, it was Aynsley Dunbar who was there. He saw me get out of the car, slightly bent over from the operation.

He ever so gently grabbed my arm for support and said, "What happened?" I told him. I knocked on my mom's door. Mom was so cute – so tiny. She greeted me with: "Well, hello patient!" I got my key and went home and crawled into bed.

Our weekends were fun. Nolan would come over on Saturday and stay overnight, then leave on Sunday to get ready for the coming workweek. One weekend, I asked him to stay Sunday for the day, but he said he had things to do. I called him later that night to see how his day was. He sounded exhausted, but I pried him for more information. He went to an art exhibit and a lady there found him quite fetching and gave him her card. I asked him what he did with the card. "I tore it in pieces." Good answer. I had a feeling he had an experience he felt tense about. We weren't engaged, but we were exclusive. And we were getting closer.

Nolan got work at an educational software company that later became Sylvan Learning. He would get up early to be at work because he called the schools on the East Coast to sell them the software. He would drink coffee and lots of it, eat Malt-O-Meal, and his nighttime meals didn't do him much good. He liked the hot stuff, the spicier the better. I often wondered if he hadn't put a hole in the lining of his stomach. Nolan developed an allergy to beer and he later turned to white wine or chardonnay.

Being a musician and living the life he did in the '70s and '80s, Nolan had the habit of staying up late and eating late. Old habits die hard, and as much as I tried to break him of that habit, I couldn't. He would come home from work, have some vino, watch the news, and then around 10:00 PM or sometimes later, we'd go get some dinner. That wasn't doing either of us any good.

His friends became my friends. There were Christmas Eve parties, birthday parties, or "any reason for a party" parties. One thing Nolan was loved for was his singing. Put a mic and a keyboard in front of him and he was in heaven. In fact, I imagine that's what he's been doing since he got over there! Life was getting interesting.

Nolan and Forrest

At this time, he lived in a guest house on the property of his friends Forrest Penner and Maria. Sometimes, he would go down to San Diego for his little sabbaticals. Then, he would call me and talk with me for a half hour. I would ask him why he had to go almost three hours away to talk to me? I often wondered if he had another family down there. When I asked him about that, he said that the didn't. He then took me to all of his favorite haunts there, with one in particular - Buca di Beppo. You know when the server has to sit down and explain the portion of the food to you, there's gotta be a problem. I was glad he trusted me enough to share his little world with me. And I was thrilled to know there weren't any little Nolans running around or even a Mrs. Nolan!

When I was getting ready to go to the Zappanale (a three-day outdoor music festival where bands from all over the world came to play Frank's music) in 2002, mom was having a hard time with me leaving. She was afraid that I wasn't coming back. Nolan spent a lot of time with her, convincing her that I would be home. In fact, I called her the day we landed and got into our rooms. I took a shower, gave her a call, and then passed out from exhaustion. Upon my arrival home, Nolan was waiting for me with a giant sunflower. When we got home, my cat Frankie exhibited behavior I've never seen a cat or dog do. It was like he was on speed. He couldn't sit still. He'd jump on the bed, move around, jump down, and run around. He made me tired just watching him. He finally calmed down and things went back to normal. This was also a time when Nolan and I were deciding what we were going to do about us. Nolan said that when I came back from Germany, if I still wanted to be with him, we'd get a place.

About this time too, Nolan was so caring and sweet when it came to my mom. He didn't have that great of a relationship with his mom, so talking with mine must have given him pleasure. They would watch TV shows together and have long talks.

We would do shopping for my mom and my brother Carl, who lived with her. Life was good, simple, sweet. And we were getting closer.

When I turned 50 in 2001, I rented a van to take my kids, their friends and me and Nolan to Vegas. We met up with a friend, Stephanie, and we hit a karaoke bar. It was a great treat to sing with and hear Nolan and Stephanie. I had lived in Vegas from 1994-1996 and met Stephanie while she was performing with a group called Capone. Jeep Capone, the great grand nephew of Al Capone, had a band that did Top 40 and they were great. I moved back to L.A. in 1996 and found an apartment on the same street my mother lived on in North Hollywood.

I had been working on the first edition of my book "My Brother Was A Mother: The Zappa Family Album," and the copies arrived at my door in 2003. It had lots of never seen family pictures and many stories of growing up with Frank and my family. It's quite an experience to see your writing in solid form. There were several book signings: one in New York, one in Lancaster, California, and another in Pomona, California. I gave one to my mom. Anyone who attended the signing in Lancaster has a real collector's item. My mom, Carl, Nolan and myself signed the books that day. In October of that year, we took mom to visit our old neighborhood in Claremont, California, and it was her last outing.

On Thanksgiving Day 2003, Nolan was going to take me, mom and Carl to meet the rest of his family. I was checking my email when Carl called and said, "Mom fell...". He might have still been talking, but that's all I heard. I told Nolan to come on, and we hurried up to her house. Mom was sitting on the bedroom floor, her back against the chest of drawers. I asked her if she hurt and she said no, but she was sorry that her fall messed up our plans. I told Carl to call paramedics, and Nolan went ahead to his family Thanksgiving dinner. There was nothing he could do there.

The wait in the hospital was long. After the X-rays came back, we were informed that mom's hip was broken. Her reaction upon hearing that news was a stoic "That's it, I'm dead." Mom was given a room and made comfortable. They scheduled her for hip surgery the next day. Up until that time, she was talking and awake.

After the surgery, she was quiet. The jostling around put her hip out of joint. She was given five milligrams of Ativan and morphine because they were going to have to pull her leg and put it back into place.

As the doctor pulled her leg gently, mom said, "ow...ow...ow" then fell asleep – for three days. On one visit, she was still asleep. I whispered in her ear that if she was over there and they told her to come home that was OK, but if she wanted to stay here and have me take care of her, that was OK too. When she came to, I was there visiting her and she had a big smile on her face. I said that we might be able to take her home, and she smiled even bigger because home to her was over there!

They transferred her to a nursing home for what they called comfort care. Other things were wrong, as her blood sugar levels and blood pressure were low. Mom was basically dying. They were trying everything to help her, but it wasn't working. I got to the nursing home and my friend Shirley and my daughter Eva were there.

The dying process is sometimes slow. Mom tried to say something to me, but she couldn't. We all sang "You Are My Sunshine" to her, and then I held her hand and watched as she quietly, gently passed. The nurse called the time at 2:20 on January 29, 2004. Ironically, the lady in the next bed, behind the curtain, started farting and not just little toots, but in the low key of C man farts. We laughed because it was just a suitable send-off for mom. She had farted a lot before the end...then the sound of a jet airplane took off and there were no airports near the nursing home. Mom took off in style to her next adventure.

I was sitting in the hallway, numb, from the whole experience. Nolan came walking towards me and I shook my head to indicate no. He said he was going to try to convince her to stay, and I said that wasn't going to happen. Nolan was very supportive and helpful with everything. Mom's funeral was beautiful and was well attended. It was a beautiful day and it had a happy feeling, as Mom was out of pain and free and with Dad and Frank.

I didn't want to stay on the same street that my mom and I lived on because there were too many sad memories. Nolan and I continued talking about moving in together. I wanted us to start anew. Joan Hudson, the wife of Nolan's friend Brian Hudson, had a property, actually a bungalow, in Echo Park, in Los Angeles, that we rented starting in November 2004. The week after we moved in, I got canned from my job at Countrywide Insurance Company. Nolan was working as an extra, so I would be getting ready to go to my new job as he would be coming home from an all-night movie shoot.

Brian Hudson and the Popular Front

While in Echo Park, Brian Hudson, Nolan, me, John Setar and Voyce McGinley worked on some of Brian's music as Brian Hudson And The Popular Front. The project was called "Condoleezza Condoleezza." We put on a show at the Backstage Coffee Gallery in Alta Dena, California. It was another large success. And again, we had a gathering of fine musicians, and Brian's songs were a hit. I loved working with Nolan. The following year, 2005, Nolan and I were both working, me at The Mortgage Store in downtown L.A., and Nolan at Westside Regional Center (WRC) in Culver City. He worked at WRC until his passing.

Above and below: a gathering to commemorate the life of my mother, Rose Marie Zappa, on February 3, 2004.

Top (l. to r.): Frank (Eva's husband), my daughter Eva, my son David, Nolan, me, my daughter Julie, and my half-sister Ann Zappa.

Bottom (l. to r.): my brother Carl, Julie, Edie Ewing, Frank (hidden in back), Mike, Larry (hidden in back), Eva, David (in front), Ann Zappa, Gay Wilson (hidden in back), Candy, Nolan, Dawn Drangle, Art Utnehmer.

Living with Nolan was good for us, but it was a culture shock for him, though. He had always said that he didn't want to lose his freedom, and living with someone hindered that. That didn't happen with me. I, of course, loved being with him, but if he got invited to go hear some music or wherever it was with friends and I didn't feel like going, I always told him to go. Nolan was in the UK several times without me, so I had to get used to being without him for even longer times. We took care of each other, and we took our vows seriously.

In October 2005, life was about to change again for us both. I was contacted by a mutual friend by email. Jim Cohen received an email from some people in England wanting to know if Nolan Porter was still alive. Jim forwarded the email to me. I responded that yes, Nolan was alive, that we lived together and who I was. The next email was an invitation to fly to Wales and participate in a show in March 2006 that they referred to as a "Weekender" at a Pontins resort. It took a second, but I replied with "Of course, we'd love to be there!" Preparations for our trip were vast and intricate. I was doing all the footwork, as I do find interest in such things like updating Nolan's passport! I was contacted by Paul Mooney, who requested to represent Nolan in the UK, and it was a sheer pleasure to meet him and maintain a working relationship with him.

The night before our departure, we spent the night at his late Aunt Bessie's house and were picked up by the shuttle and dropped off at LAX. We were both a bundle of nerves since it had been a long time since either of us had flown anywhere, let alone the UK! We left on Wednesday afternoon, with a layover in Pennsylvania, and arrived at Heathrow Airport on Thursday morning. We were then driven to Wales and settled in our room. It was so beautiful there, but a cold 10 degrees!

One day we had off and a bunch of the performers and us went on a four-hour trip to London. It was something that I wish had been recorded! Somebody was telling some randy stories, and that whole bus was screaming with laughter, so I joined in and told a couple myself!

I had told Nolan to practice his signature because he was going to be asked for it on all sorts of things. He didn't believe it until we were seated at dinner and a line of people came with their programs and quite respectfully asked for his autograph. He was signing for a long time, amazed all the while! Nolan was so popular there and he was in awe of it all. I was too, and I was thrilled to be a part of it.

The rehearsal followed that day, and it was great hearing all of the other groups there: Dean Parrish, Doni Burdick, The Precisions, Lou Ragland, Caroline Crawford, and many other groups. The next night, when Nolan came on stage, it was huge. I mean, the girlfriends and wives of the performers

Nolan performing in Prestatyn, Wales.

were in the nosebleed section atop the bleachers, and the sound of the yelling and applause was thunderous up there! There were about thirty-five hundred people gathered and it may have been cold outside, but inside that room it was eighty-five degrees! I was sad to have it end, but the next day we took a train to Sherwood Forest – yes, THE Sherwood Forest, and we met up with our friend Robert Wigley. We took a walk through the forest and saw the actual tree Robin Hood and Maid Marion hid in from the Sheriff of Nottingham.

This page: Nolan and I at Sherwood Forest.

Top left: Nolan has found the bathroom in the forest!

Top right: Thanks to the assistance of friend and Zappa fanatic Lou Allred, the "Second Chance" CD was informally sold at "Once A Legacy" shows starting in 2006. Although not in the official Nolan Porter discography, this disc (and our promotional VHS tape) generated more interest in our talents and it became an essential part of our musical and personal growth.

Below: Nolan performing during his cruise ship days.

Nolan and the rest of the crew on board.

Nolan performed in many places besides the US and the UK. During the '80s, he was in Bali, Singapore, and had a three-month gig in Alaska. He worked on cruise ships, and one of the ships he was on had caught fire.

Nolan and I met lots of people once he started performing overseas in 2006. This photo is during our trip in Prestatyn, Wales.

At right is another photo from the Pontins resort in Wales. The woman sitting next to me is Jeanne Sorenson.

That's the one and only Motorhead Sherwood in our midst!

Lou Allred could throw some Zappa-themed parties! From his 2006 shindig, we have: (l. to r. - back row) Mark Enevoldson, Wally Salazar, me, Motorhead Sherwood, Denny Walley, Tom Leavey, John French, Doug Moon, Nolan; (l. to r. front row) Johnny Franklin, Peter Lovio, Frank Salazar.

At one point, Nolan was even in my brother Frank's house, on Woodrow Wilson Drive, with his producer/agent Gabriel Mekler. Nolan got around. We must have crossed paths many times but didn't know it. While he was busy entertaining in those exotic places, I was holding down the fort in the San Fernando Valley performing at various clubs and getting my own notoriety. I loved performing like Nolan did, so when we finally got together, it was no wonder we ended up singing together.

It was a cold January morning in 2007. Nolan was standing at the wall heater warming his back. We had talked about marriage, and he didn't know how to go about asking me. I was sitting at the computer busy with issues about our upcoming move. All of sudden, he came over to me and got down on one knee and said, "What am I waiting for? Will you marry me?" It took me by surprise and I never miss an opportunity to inject humor into a tense moment, so I said, "Oh yes, and it's going to cost so much money!" He came back with: "Well, don't scare me!"

We hugged and kissed and I was so happy! We moved to the San Fernando Valley into an apartment. That year, we were married on April 28 and 29. How is that you say? Well, the day of the wedding, there was a lot of activity, and silly me, I forgot to bring the paperwork with me. We still were married, but I had to bring the paperwork the next day to have it signed. So, we got to celebrate two days for our anniversary. We decided on a Las Vegas

Three photos from our wedding day at an Elvis chapel in Las Vegas. As you can see, the guy who married us was not an Elvis impersonator!

wedding, and my daughters Julie and Eva and Eva's husband Frank were there as was my sister Ann and friends Cindy and Terry Pruitt, Carey and Gary Reedy, and Nolan's mother Estell. We were both so happy to finally be married. We had a marvelous time and it was our luckiest time on the slot machines!

In 2008, I had surgery on my hand and elbow, and Nolan was a great help to me. That was also the start of our financial stress. Money was a constant concern for Nolan, and at one point, his job was not paying anyone for three weeks. Things worked out, and by 2010 we were back on track. Nolan was getting ready to go over to the UK again for another music tour, this time with the band Stone Foundation. Neil Sheasby and Neil Jones hit it off with Nolan, and he was there for a couple of weeks. A couple years later, Nolan was in a short documentary made by Lee Cogswell called "Keep On Keepin' On" about his interactions with Stone Foundation. As I watch it, it's like Nolan is still here talking to me! The second version of my book "My Brother Was A Mother: Take 2," was released in 2011. I included fan recollections of meeting Frank, pictures, and other memorabilia.

Highlights from the 2010 tour (top photo courtesy of Frank Cleverley).

In the CKCU-FM 93.1 studio in Ottawa for Bobby Marquis' "Pure Radio Kaos" program in 2012.

We were flown to Ottawa, Ontario, Canada in 2012 to perform for a fundraiser for prostate cancer, in honor of Frank. The radio show we did took place on the 28th of November, and we played at a club called Irene's on December 1. We met many wonderful friends, including Bobby Marquis, as well as Guy Short, who played sax in the band The Boogiemen that backed us up. One friend in particular was a young lady named Patty Gunderson. She was there on that Monday night just out having a drink with a friend, and we got to meet her. She knew nothing of Frank. I know that amazed me too, but she didn't, and after Nolan and I came home, Patty and I continued our friendship. I discovered a talent she had that was quite amazing. She channeled people who passed on. One day, we were talking and she said Frank was there. I was kind of shocked, but she continued and through Patty, Frank told me things only I would know. Frank apologized, saying he wished he had helped me more in my music endeavors, and I said there was nothing to apologize for as he had a life to live and make music in. Later on, I would find out that Patty was able to channel Nolan.

Below and on the next page are photos from a Nolan Porter/ Stone Foundation gig on July 8, 2012 at The Musician in Leicester, UK. The photos are courtesy of John Coles.

Below are two photos from a gig at the unfortunately named Uncle Tom's Cabin in Blackpool, England on July 14, 2012.

with Neil Jones

On this page are highlights from Nolan's appearance with Stone Foundation at Guilfest in Guildford, England on July 15, 2012. They played on the final day of this three-day festival.

with drummer Phil Ford

with Neil Jones

"Keep On Keepin' On," Lee Cogswell's film about Nolan's 2012 UK tour with Stone Foundation, debuted on June 22, 2013. It included performance footage from the stage and the studio, as well as exclusive interviews with Nolan and members of the band.

When I had back surgery in 2014, Nolan brought me home. He would help me to the bathroom, bring me stuff to eat, etc. I asked my daughter Julie to come out from Colorado and help me for a week. As you can see from the ads on the right, Nolan had another trip to the UK that year, so he was doing well musically.

As it turned out, everything in the past was just an appetizer. During the summer 2014 tour with Stone Foundation, Nolan would reach heights that neither he nor the band had experienced before. They played just four gigs, but one of them was London's 100 Club, at which Nolan had recorded a live album with the band in 2012. In addition, a live band set was recorded for "The Craig Charles Funk And Soul Show" for BBC Radio 6, and Nolan and Stone Foundation's guitarist/leader Neil Jones went to BBC Birmingham to record an acoustic set and interview.

Nolan ripping it up at The 100 Club in London on July 24, 2014.

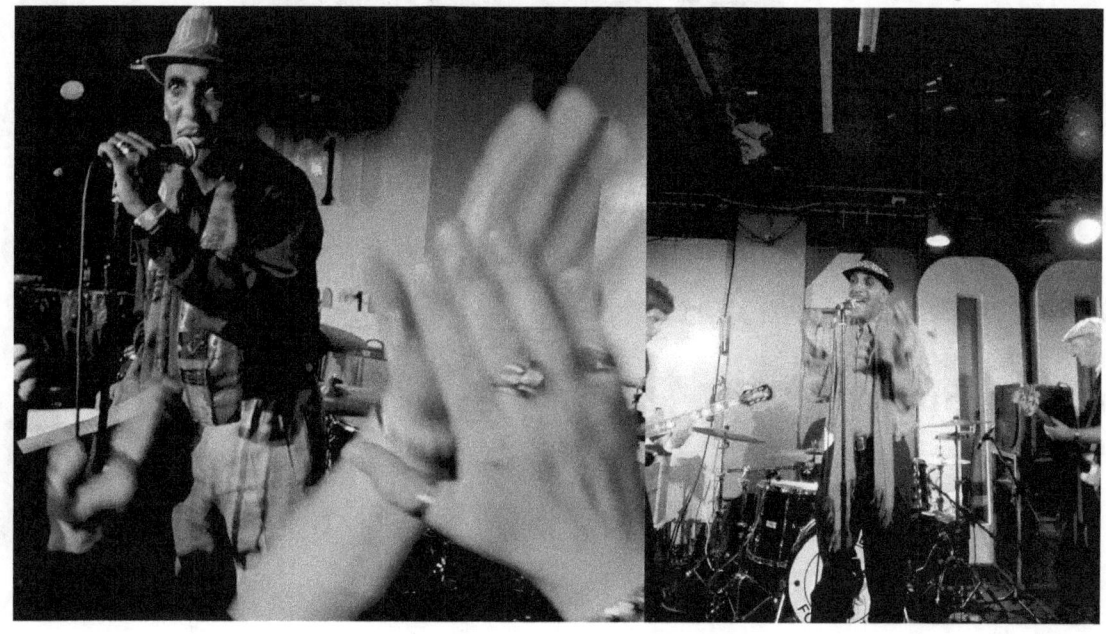

Left: at The Globe in Cardiff, Wales (July 25, 2014).

with Neil Sheasby and Neil Jones

Backstage at The 100 Club.

No, your eyes are not playing tricks on you! This out of focus shot perfectly captures the dazed and confused conditions of Neil Jones, Nolan and Neil Sheasby on the tour bus!

Top right: Nolan teaching Neil Sheasby's sons how to fist up for protection!

Middle left: Nolan and Stone Foundation flying to Spain for the wonderfully named Euro Ye Ye Festival!

Middle right: Nolan and Neil Jones at BBC Birmingham, and below that, the full band at BBC Radio 6 Music studios.

Bottom left: another BBC Radio 6 shot.

Bottom right: Jones and Nolan in Spain.

Top and bottom: It's amazing what you'll find in Birmingham, UK!

Middle left: as you can probably tell, this shot was considered an outtake!

Middle right: Nolan with Neil Jones and Neil Sheasby.

Nolan was a very soulful man, intuitive and gracious. He had so many friends that loved him, and that fact always humbled him. Women just loved him, and his male friends, well, they loved him too. I have no doubt that wherever he is now, he is loved beyond words.

Nolan wrote about recent happenings in early 2015:

"Hello all, this is my first letter of 2015. What can I say? It's been a hard year, it's been a good year, it's been a great year! Some of you were wondering, which is it? Hey, it's all good. The hard part was watching my very talented and supportive wife wince in absolute pain if she walked more than 10 feet or stood on stage for more than one song. The good part of the year started right after Patrice's surgery in April. When I saw that she could stand up straight and walk a city block without bending over in abject pain, I was overjoyed. Patrice was even happier. I credit lots of prayer and good science for her healing and recovery. The year got even better as I prepared to tour the English and Welsh countryside with the great Stone Foundation – as fine a bunch of mates and musicians as I've ever traveled with. The performances at The 100 Club, The Musician and the BBC, were magic, and our time in the studio inspiring. Thanks, Stone Foundation.

"Not only did various band members share the stage with me, they shared their families and their homes with me. English hospitality is a fine tradition, indeed! I've been so lucky getting to know my UK mates through the eyes and ears of creativity and music. On my travels through towns, hamlets and large cities (Birmingham, London) and a few choice taverns, I've met some very cool and soulful people. Long live soul music, long live and God bless the UK.

"2014 ended on a very positive note, musically speaking. I released both my albums on a single CD by Crossfire Publications and Porterville Records. I'll bet a lot of you that bought my albums in the early '70s have nothing to play them on, now with so few turntables around. Some of the mixes sound noticeably better than some of the analog recordings. I owe quite a lot to Greg Russo, author of "Cosmik Debris" fame. Not only has he written the best book to date about Frank Zappa, but has also shown his hand as a very talented producer, songwriter/engineer, and friend. Greg spent hundreds of hours remixing and getting the very brightest and crispest sounds that these recordings have at present, and it was a real labor of love! Thanks, Greg.

"As most of you have seen or heard by now, barely a week into the new year, free speech was attacked in Paris, and people were targeted and attacked for merely being identified as Jewish. How tragic. How sad. Let us not forget that one Islamic man gave his life trying to protect Charlie Hebdo's staff. It was a very brave young man who happened to be a Muslim who saved the lives of several patrons at the kosher market in Paris by guiding them to safety inside a storage unit.

"It continues to be my hope that art and music will continue to be a bridge that we can all cross in both directions, and in crossing, learn more about each other, learn to care more for one another, and realize that there is more that binds us together than separates us."

"I love you all, Keep On Keepin' On. Je Suis Charlie, Je Suis Juif, Je Suis Nolan."

Nolan was a good Jew. He took it all very seriously. His faith guided him through some tough times in his life. He told me when he went before the Beit Din, a panel of four rabbis who ask questions, one question he was asked was why he wanted to convert to Judaism. Nolan's answer was that it felt like home, like a family. We were active in our temple services. We both converted to Judaism: Nolan in the 1980s, and me in 2015. Our Rabbi Jerry Cutler and his family, Rebbetzin Jefferson and daughters Chelsea and Tess, made everyone feel at home. Jerry's sermons were the best. Our Sabbath services were great, and we would perform songs for the congregation. Some of our best performances were on those nights. Sometimes, it seemed that Nolan was losing confidence in his singing. I would tell him that he was as good as ever and that nothing was changing. I loved his voice and he loved mine, and that's why we blended so well together when we sang. When he was on tour in the UK several times, when he was on stage, he was the best. He would shake his money maker, as I liked to call it, and sing his heart out. The crowd loved him. No shortage of applause, whistles and yells! He loved to play his keyboards and often wished he could play better. I told him he could if he wanted to, to just practice. He was very inventive in chord progressions and style. I regret not having worked more with him, and that's on me. I am an impatient person, and I can start singing and work through a song. Nolan would stop me so he could get the keyboard part right. A slow-moving Taurus and a quick let's-get-on-with-it triple Aries...oh my.

I was invited to perform at the Zappanale in Bad Doberan, Germany in 2016,

Above/below: Nolan and I with King Cotton at the 5th Messaround concert at Viva Cantina, Burbank, CA (February 15, 2015; photos by E.L. Woody).

34

and Nolan came with me. It had been 14 years since the first Zappanale I attended in 2002. There was a lot of catching up to do, so I told the audience about my book "My Brother Was A Mother: The Zappa Family Album" plus the updated editions which I happened to have with me if anyone was interested! I also mentioned that my mother passed away in 2004 and that I had married a man of color, and maybe they might know him, Nolan Porter! The crowd cheered and Nolan came onstage, smiling from ear to ear. We sang one of his songs, "If I Could Only Be Sure," and it was well received. Did I mention that they loved Nolan?

Below: Nolan with Julie.

Below: Dr. Dot made a house call!

Above: the brain trust of the Porter/Zappa operation meets at the famous Stop 20 Diner in Elmont, New York! This meeting, which took place on September 27, 2016, featured (left to right): Larry Rogak, Nolan, me, Carmen Pagán, Greg Russo.
(Photo by Rita Russo)

We also took a trip in September 2016 to see my brother Bob and his wife Diane. Bob was earlier diagnosed with amyloidosis and he also told me to get tested for it, as his doctor thought our father may have had it and passed it on. I found out that I carry the latent T3 gene, but all of my tests came out normal. Little did I know that our trip would be the last time we would see Bob. On December 8th at 1:00 AM, I received a call from Diane's daughter Anna saying that Bob had passed away. Nolan and I had a show to do later that night, and I announced the passing of Bob and dedicated the show to him.

In 2018, we were both flown to Blackpool, UK for another show at the Winter Gardens. Nolan performed and I was lucky enough to be able to sing with the background singers while he was onstage! That was a fabulous trip. Our lodging was across the street from the Irish Sea, a majestic body of water with so much strength in it. It was also the first time Nolan experienced vertigo. He was scheduled to do a Q&A that morning, but he was too ill to attend. I also met another promoter, Hitsville Chalky, while there. He's a very nice man, and in fact, the British folks are a grand lot – very friendly and funny!

We went back for my third Zappanale in July 2019. This time, I sang a couple of Frank's songs with Ed Palermo's Big Band and that was the second time I sang with them since 2002. Both times were fabulous, and now they are a not so distant memory.

At right is a photo of when we were hanging out at Zappanale. On the left is Angel Tejeda, founder of a Mexican fan club for Zappa fans.

Nolan was about serving and helping people. The place where he worked for 16 years, Westside Regional Center, did just that, helping people with disabilities coupled with mental challenges to lead a good life. Nolan was surrounded by caring social workers and other case aides that he loved, and they loved him. Some of these people can be seen in the "Behind the Scenes" section of this book.

In October 2019, Nolan was flown across the pond to tour with a group called The Signatures. Their drummer Gavin Creates-Webb and his wife Sharon took care of Nolan's trip. Nolan made more friends on this trip, the band loved him, and they sounded solid together.

While there on tour, a video of Nolan performing was sent to me and I noticed that he seemed to be swimming in the shirt he was wearing. It was so large and he looked smaller in it. When he came home, he had lost some weight, but I thought that I'd fatten him up with my cooking. He loved my fried chicken, pasta, salads, chili...I was cooking up a storm and he was eating. It almost looked as if he was gaining a few pounds.

2020 reared its ugly head and the fucking pandemic hit. My sweet man was masking up with gloves and bucking a heavy unhealthy wind, shopping for foodstuffs, and whatever he could get that the other plagues of locusts hadn't already snapped up. He would come

Thanks to fan Carlo Didcott for these two photos from Nolan's gig on October 11, 2019 at The Tavern in Melton Mowbray, Leicestershire, England. Nolan was backed by The Signatures for this run of shows. Additional photos from Carlo taken at the next evening's gig at The Live Rooms in Chester follow on the next six pages.

home with boxes of stuff, ten-pound bags of potatoes and rice and hand sanitizer, masks, but no toilet paper. That soon became a scarcity. That's what I loved about Nolan, among many things, he cared for us and took care of me. He was always making sure I had money in my pocket, food in the pantry and refrigerator, and gas in the car.

Celebrating my birthday with Nolan and Julie.

We enjoyed our weekend trips and his last year was great. Now that I think of it, I believe he knew he was dying, but he wanted me to have a good time before he left. He would always say, "If I pass before my mother" (she's in her 90s) and I would say that he wouldn't. It's kind of a self-fulfilling prophecy. We would come up to Ventura almost every weekend and have a great time. But I could see that he was trying to hide his pain.

Around late May or early June, Nolan awoke vomiting and in a lot of stomach pain. I made him some peppermint tea and waited to see if that would help soothe him. I had to go to work, and as I got to the door, he turned his head to look at me and said: "I love you with all my heart." I told him I loved him too and added that if he needed me, I would come

home. He called about 1:30 and told me he needed me, and like Mario Andretti, I raced home. I told him to get dressed and we were going to Urgent Care. They took him in and his blood pressure was 200 something over 100 something and that landed him in the emergency room. Of course, with the stinking COVID thing, I was not permitted to sit and wait for him. After about four hours, I picked him up and that's when he told me they found a mass on his liver.

At first, they thought it was his adrenal gland. The "doctor" that was assigned to Nolan, quite matter-of-factly stated that, "Oh yeah, I can take it out." Surgery was scheduled for August 12. The worry that Nolan went through plummeted his weight to 129 pounds, and at 5'11", he looked like a Holocaust survivor. I was with him from start to finish. I was there while they prepared him for surgery, I watched as they wheeled him in, and I sat in the waiting room. It was freezing in there and I thought about taking a nap. As I laid there, a nurse came in and laid a warm blanket on me. What a sweet gesture. After what seemed an eternity, the "doctor" came in and mumbled something about how he couldn't remove the tumor, then abruptly turned and walked away. I was stunned because we were led to believe it would be over and maybe we could think about getting grey hair together while sitting on the porch of our new place watching the sunset. 'Twas not to be.

With Julie at The Mediterranean Grill, Ventura, California.

In the recovery room, Nolan awoke to the worst news that his tumor couldn't be removed. He looked like he lost his best friend. The "doctor" said there were blood vessels wrapped around it and it was beyond his expertise, so he decided not to attempt it. That little decision there might have saved what was left of Nolan's life. In fact, he was told later, by a member of the so-called doctor's staff, that it was better that he didn't proceed with the operation.

In the meantime, it was suggested that we get a second opinion at another hospital, a place that dealt in just such issues. Before doing that, however, Nolan was scheduled for a tumor biopsy in October. It was a success, but Nolan's health just took a downward spiral after that. We spent his last Thanksgiving at the home of Diane Green, a longtime friend, and I'm glad we did. He hadn't been really seeing anyone for a while, and they were ecstatic to see him, even if he was in a wheelchair.

Diane Green with Nolan on Thanksgiving.

Nolan knew he was sick and we talked about his care. He said he should go to a hospital, but I said no, and that I would take care of him. I had taken care of my mother before she passed, so I was used to the long hours and the stress of it. Nolan took care of me when I had my back operation, and now it was my turn. Only I got better…he wouldn't.

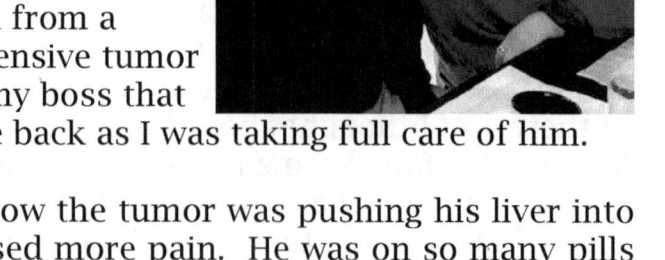

Also, by now we had received the second opinion from a wonderful real doctor who prescribed a very expensive tumor shrinking medication. I was working, but I told my boss that once Nolan was on that medication, I wouldn't be back as I was taking full care of him.

The side effects of the drug were horrible, and now the tumor was pushing his liver into his diaphragm, causing hiccups that in turn caused more pain. He was on so many pills that one day he told me his head was swimming from all of them. I felt so bad, but he had to take them. December was a hard month.

January 2021

The palliative care team came to check on Nolan every week, bathing him, and checking his vitals. That was always good. Then one morning, we both woke up and I asked him how he was feeling. By this time, his verbal noises were usually grunts or nods, but this morning he looked at me with a look of "This is it." Needless to say, I was scared and phoned the head nurse to discuss a few things. Later that morning, he jumped out of bed and fell, hitting his head. I was told that if he fell, to leave him there and call 911 for "an assist lift" as I wasn't able to get him back in bed. The next day, he was put in hospice, bathed, changed clothes and put into the hospital bed they brought out. Now, the pain was more than just a moan. Morphine was a constant thing for him, in addition to meds for nausea and anxiety. My daughter Julie came on of her many days, and while the nurses were there, she showed them bed sores on Nolan that they had sadly neglected. He got daily care after that, and much better care, too.

Friends and family came by the weekend before he passed and brought food. I talked to Nolan and I was numb. Julie told me she would take care of me, and to be quite honest, I hadn't even thought of what I was going to do after he passed. Now I knew I had a place to go. Thank you, Julie. Nights were hard, because after I got done cleaning Nolan and medicating him, I was exhausted. I would just get to sleep when he would call out to me or in pain. A good friend of Nolan's, José Rendon, would come by around 11:30 and stay all night with Nolan while I got some sleep.

February 1-3, 2021

I can't remember these days. I asked Nolan not to leave, if he could stay for another day.

February 4, 2021

Nolan's longtime friend David Glasband and Julie were there with me to tend to Nolan.

The evening had quieted down. At around 7:30, I went to sit with Nolan for what would be my last time.

He had his head turned towards me and I looked into those beautiful eyes and told him that I loved him with all my heart and he was the best man I ever had. I said I would be OK and it was time to let go. As I said that, I could feel his heartbeat stop, and the breathing, though shallow, stopped too. He was at peace – no more pain or worry. His heart and soul stepped into the next realm, and it was done.

The day after Nolan passed, our Canadian friend Patty Gunderson told me that Nolan had already reached out to her and said to tell me he loved me to the moon and back. He would say that to me while he was still here. In the Jewish tradition when a person dies, there is a ritual called the Tahara where the body is washed, prayed over, dressed in white pajamas and then a shroud and placed in a simple pine box. I asked Patty what Nolan looked like, and she said he's young, healthy and he's "rocking those white pajamas." I never told her about the pajamas. She also said he was wearing a fedora-type hat with a feather in it. Oh, if only I could see a picture! Patty helped me understand a lot of things, and I'll always be grateful.

The young man from the hospital came out to declare him. The ladies from the mortuary came and gently, respectfully wrapped him in cloth, put him in the hearse, and took him to the mortuary for the traditional Jewish ceremony called the Tahara.

February 8, 2021

A very nice gathering of friends and family attended Nolan's funeral at Ivy Lawn Cemetery in Ventura, and it was presided over by our Rabbi Jerry Cutler. It was a good ceremony, but it was cold! Some of us had lunch afterwards and had a great time, as Nolan would have wanted it. There were hundreds of responses to Nolan's passing. Some of them are shown here. I was on the phone day and night. It was good to talk to everyone knowing how much Nolan was loved and that they cared how I was doing.

And another chapter of my life ends, and another begins.

March 16, 2021

Julie's friend Patrick came and picked up me and Chewy, my cat, and we drove away from the Valley for the last time. It was bittersweet to say goodbye to memories of life with Nolan, but knowing I was going to live in a bigger, cleaner place by the beach, oh, that was irresistible. My tears soon turned into dry eyes as I watched the scenery that Nolan and I drove by so many times on our way to visit Ventura and Julie. Now, I was coming here alone, but not really, as I would be living in Julie's home. Nolan is here, so we're all together as I always wanted.

One day, I was sitting at the computer looking at Nolan's pictures. It came to me to put this book together, and a friend offered to have me record at his studio any songs I wanted.

I know there are those of you who don't believe in an afterlife or messages from "beyond," but I can confirm they do exist. I was afraid of dying when I was younger, and it's not a pleasant thought when you don't know what's "beyond the sky." Actually, "the other side" isn't up there; it's actually about two feet above the ground. If you ever read someone's account of seeing a spirit or "ghost" floating, it's because they're two feet off the ground. Now keep in mind these ideas are not mine solely, but I have read much on the afterlife and what goes on. The late Sylvia Browne provides mass information on this subject, and I highly recommend reading her books.

My friend Patty MacGillivray told me that Nolan just reached out already! He is really busy and overwhelmed with everything. He said, "Tell Patrice that everything is just great! It's wild!" Patty has been a really good, true friend and I am grateful for her gift of being able to channel Nolan for me. Being a widow isn't easy, but I have a link to him. Of course, I get messages from him too, like the time I was in my credit union taking care of business…the first song we ever sang together came on the speaker. There's a white butterfly that comes by almost every day outside the upstairs kitchen window. I just know he's here.

If you have lost someone close to you, look for signs. My mom would leave change on the floor. I would find pennies, dimes and nickels all the time. In fact, the night she passed my electricity, lights, and TV went plooky! That's one of the first things you might notice. When my father passed, the heater would go on by itself because he was always cold. His circulation was poor and he always had cold hands and feet while sitting on the sofa with a blanket around him, watching TV. My brother Bob's wife Diane tells me about all the signs Bob leaves for her - the knocking, lights flickering, etc. She wrote a book about her time with him, "The Married Widow." Bob passed in 2018.

Nolan always told me he didn't know if there was an afterlife. He knows it now! From what Patty has told me, he's a very happy soul! I just miss him very much.

Nolan and I have lost many friends and family over these 22 years. He lost his Aunt Bessie, his grandmother Esther, uncle Jonathan, cousins, and other friends. I've lost all my brothers, Frank, Bob and Carl, and sister Ann. Numerous friends that will always be in my heart. The hardest one to lose was Nolan himself.

I know there's a heaven, and Nolan's up there working with some of the best musicians and artists. I'll see if I can add to it when I get there. Until then, hold a place for me, Nolan. I love you with all my heart or as you used to tell me, to the moon and back.

Nolan and I at Catasonic Studios in L.A. (photo courtesy of Mark Wheaton).

WHERE IT ALL STARTED

Let's go all the way back to the beginning to see what happened to Nolan musically before I came into the picture. Greg Russo can help us with that...

Nolan Frederick Porter II was born in Los Angeles, California on May 10, 1949. Nolan took in and enjoyed both R&B and rock while growing up in the L.A. area. He started writing when he was 10, and began performing a couple years later. While attending Los Angeles High School, Nolan Porter honed his singing and songwriting skills. After his graduation, Porter began performing live in a madrigal group at Los Angeles City College in late 1968. Mani Mekler, the sister of Steppenwolf and Three Dog Night producer Gabriel Mekler, was also part of that madrigal group. Mani introduced Nolan to Gabriel. Mekler had produced a major hit with Steppenwolf's "Born To Be Wild" earlier in 1968, so this was a great break for Nolan to be involved with a hot record producer.

Gabriel Mekler arranged for Nolan to do a demo session on February 13, 1969 at American Recorders in Studio City, California. Richard Podolor was the engineer. This wasn't just any demo session - Steppenwolf's Jerry Edmonton (born Jerry McCrohan) and Goldy St. John (John Goadsby) were on hand to provide drums and keyboards, respectively. They recorded Nolan's song "Don't Make Me Color My Black Face Blue" and "The Fifth One" by David Blue (aka Stuart David Cohen). This was typical of the R&B/rock mixture that Nolan immersed himself in. After this session, Nolan Porter was offered a record deal by Gabriel Mekler. Gabriel did not have a record label at the time, but he was in the process of setting one up. The promise of Nolan Porter's demo session set Mekler's label plans into motion. Sadly, the tapes for these demos are nowhere to be found today.

Nolan recalled this about "The Fifth One": "It was a song that Gabriel really liked, and he knew David Blue. What I liked about the song was the lyrics, and I didn't know if it was a love song or a religious song." Porter's genesis of "Don't Make Me Color My Black Face Blue" was more direct: "I was infatuated with a woman ten years older than me who knew how to play me like a fiddle, but she wasn't a bad sort. She was just smarter than I was, and I resented it!"

It took Nolan a year to finally hit the recording studio again. Nolan revealed why: "Actually, I didn't have my act together. I was in transition from a trained musical stage singer to a pop singer. The methods were different. Gabriel Mekler was my music teacher, friend, and mentor."

When Gabriel Mekler got his own act together, he formed the Lizard Records label. Starting January 1, 1970, Lizard's releases would be pressed and distributed by the tape manufacturer Ampex, which had a label of its own. Porter and Mekler agreed that Nolan would record tracks for Lizard and that Mekler would produce and release them under different names to combat discrimination by radio stations. Mekler's thinking was that if one of the subsequent records released as Nolan, N.F. Porter or Frederick II was a hit, Nolan Porter would perform under that name.

Mekler reached out to drummer Jimmy Carl Black, who was recently unemployed by Frank

Zappa's breakup of the original Mothers Of Invention.

According to Jimmy, "I was given the job of putting together the band for Nolan Porter to record with. Little did I know that they would go off on their own as Little Feat!" Jimmy played on Nolan's first three recording sessions with fellow MOI members Roy Estrada on bass and guitarist Lowell George (previously of the Uni group The Factory) along with sax/conga player Tony Elisalda and three seasoned backing vocalists later known as The Blackberries: former Raelettes vocalist Clydie King, former Ikettes member Venetta Fields, and Sherlie Matthews. In addition to producing, Gabriel Mekler also served as the band's keyboardist.

With all this talent around him, Nolan was very impressed: "It was a great learning experience for me, since all the guys were seasoned players and performers and I was just starting my recording career. It was great working with Clydie, Venetta and Sherlie because they brought experience from other groups they had performed with, like The Raelettes, The Beatles, and Phil Spector. Of course, I can't forget the guys in Little Feat - in addition to working with Lowell George, the great Bill Payne, keyboardist extraordinaire, also worked with us."

At the band's first Wally Heider Recording session in Hollywood during the second week of March 1970, they re-recorded the two songs from Nolan's demo session. These were followed up by a cover of Van Morrison's "Crazy Love" and Nolan's tune with Leno Francen, called "What Would You Do If I Did That To You." Mekler asked Steppenwolf to record "What Would You Do..." for their "Monster" album released in November 1969, but Nolan didn't receive anything from that gold-selling LP. Nolan remembered this about the song: "Leno Francen was a good friend of Gabriel and myself, and he was the perfect co-writer for the song." The third session covered Nolan's R&B shaker "Fe-Fi-Fo-Fum" and Leno Francen's "Gwendolyn." "Fe-Fi-Fo-Fum" was about the differences between Nolan's generation and his father's generation. For "Gwendolyn," Nolan took a different approach to get in the mood: "I saw the film 'Becket' starring Richard Burton and Peter O'Toole. The relationship between the king, his best friend and his best friend's wife, Gwendolyn, was moving and inspiring." Nolan continued to prove that he was equally adept at navigating material that crossed the R&B, rock, and pop idioms.

Following the first three sessions, there was a two-week break. Jimmy Carl Black wished to form his own group called Geronimo Black (named after his son). To fulfill his obligation to Gabriel Mekler and Nolan Porter, Jimmy replaced himself in the band with Factory drummer Richie Hayward and keyboardist Bill Payne. A few months later, Hayward and Payne would record three tracks with Lowell George to prepare them for their next project - Little Feat. Of this recording arrangement, Nolan thought: "It was the best. How could I be so lucky as to have musicians from Frank Zappa and Little Feat?" The initial Geronimo Black lineup soon fell apart. Since Jimmy Carl Black had already turned over the reins to Hayward and Payne, he couldn't come back.

Nolan's revised lineup did three more sessions at Wally Heider's studio at the end of March 1970. The first of these tracked Porter's "Travelin' Song" and Randy Newman's "Let's Burn Down The Cornfield." Looking back at "Travelin' Song," Nolan recalled: "It was a song about searching for true love, looking all over the world and finding it my own backyard, so to speak." Nolan also provided information about Randy Newman's tune as well: "It's a ritual in Africa to burn down the cornfields in hopes of a better crop next year. Randy Newman's manager heard my version and passed a message to me that he and Randy thought it was interesting and they liked it!"

Next up were the Stax classic "Iron Out The Rough Spots" and overdubs for "Fe-Fi-Fo-Fum." Don Covay originally recorded "Iron Out The Rough Spots," which was written by Stax's standout session men Steve Cropper, Booker T. Jones, and David Porter (no relation). Covay's powerful vocal on the song inspired Nolan to do his own take on it. Lowell George and Bill Payne completed their work with Nolan Porter by writing a song for him: "Somebody's Gone." The song was never re-recorded by Lowell George or Little Feat. A song dealing with times gone by, "Somebody's Gone" was perfectly suited for Nolan. In fact, Nolan recalled: "Lowell told me that he wrote it especially for me because we both loved the art scene in Venice Beach near Santa Monica. Venice Beach was the center of the world. It was fun and a little dangerous, and the song reflects that. Yeah, it was special."

Mekler got things going by releasing (via Lizard) the Nolan single "Crazy Love"/ "What Would You Do If I Did That To You" in late May 1970. Since other artists had recorded and released Van Morrison's "Crazy Love" as a single, the competition resulted in no one having a hit with the song. "Crazy Love" had a powerful effect on Nolan: "I heard the song and just wanted to record it because I thought the melody was beautiful and it represented the type of love I was looking for at the time."

The album that Nolan Porter and Gabriel Mekler were recording required one more song. In early June 1970, Mekler took Nolan to The Sound Factory in Hollywood with an almost entirely different band. The only holdovers were sax and percussion man Tony Elisalda and the three backing vocalists. At this point, Mekler went with a revolving door of higher caliber session musicians to give Porter's recordings an even brighter sheen. This time, keyboardist Clarence McDonald, bassist William Allen, drummer Sanford Konikoff and guitarist David T. Walker did the honors. Nolan's gospel-influenced "Somebody's Cryin'" maximized his talents and those of the other participants. Another version of "Somebody's Cryin'" was recorded live at The Troubadour in L.A. on June 15, 1970. Since Tony Elisalda could not play sax and congas at a live gig, Robert Torres was brought in to play Tony's recorded sax arrangement. Porter recounted this about "Somebody's Cryin'": "Gabriel thought we should record it live at The Troubadour and in the studio, and that we should compare the two. It made sense to me, as the song was about comparing one thing to another."

Nolan recalled that things were going very quickly and the best musicians were always in demand: "I think what was going on at that time was that we were working with musicians who were very successful in their own right and very busy. We had a certain window of

Gabriel Mekler's Lizard Records label got Nolan's first album title wrong – it should have been punctuated as "Nolan – No Apologies." In Nolan's view, the album title was supposed to appear as a signoff to a deeply personal letter that he was writing to someone special in his life.

In the original print ad that appeared in the June 27, 1970 edition of Billboard magazine, the section "What the Critics Are Saying" was in very small print. However, what those critics said was absolutely fascinating, even at this early stage in Nolan's career:

"Nolan Porter is the most exciting male singer I've heard since the world first discovered Mick Jagger."

"There is magic in this debut album. It's the kind of record you can't help but respond to on both a physical and emotional level."

"...Certain to be one of the most important new singers in the wide field of popular music."

"The most compelling feature of Nolan's vocal performances is his astounding versatility. On different cuts, you can detect some of the flamboyance of James Brown, the soul of Otis Redding, the poetics of Donovan, and the clean joyous economy of John Sebastian. But for overall feeling, I have to say that Nolan evokes the same kind of raw response that I first got from Ray Charles before he made the switch to country and western."
— Chris Van Ness

opportunity to work with them. When that window was closed, we had to find other players just as good. Also, Gabriel was a perfectionist. He may have thought a player was really good, but not right for that song. So, we made some changes. I was transforming from being a college student, hippie wanderer and player to being a serious recording artist. I didn't have much experience traveling on the road with other musicians, but I had a lot of great musicians brought to me by Gabriel Mekler. I was more interested in honing my skills with these more mature musicians than traveling at the time. L.A. was my musical playground, and The Troubadour was one of the best places to play."

Nolan's album "Nolan - No Apologies" was issued on Lizard in late June 1970. As mentioned on the previous page, mistakes throughout the album's packaging and promotion led everyone to believe that the artist's name was Nolan and the album was simply called "No Apologies." As the link between Lowell George's time with The Factory and the formation of Little Feat, "Nolan - No Apologies" helped Lowell George, Bill Payne, Roy Estrada and Richie Hayward to land their own Little Feat record deal with Warner Bros. Released with a small amount of promotion, "Nolan - No Apologies" sold poorly.

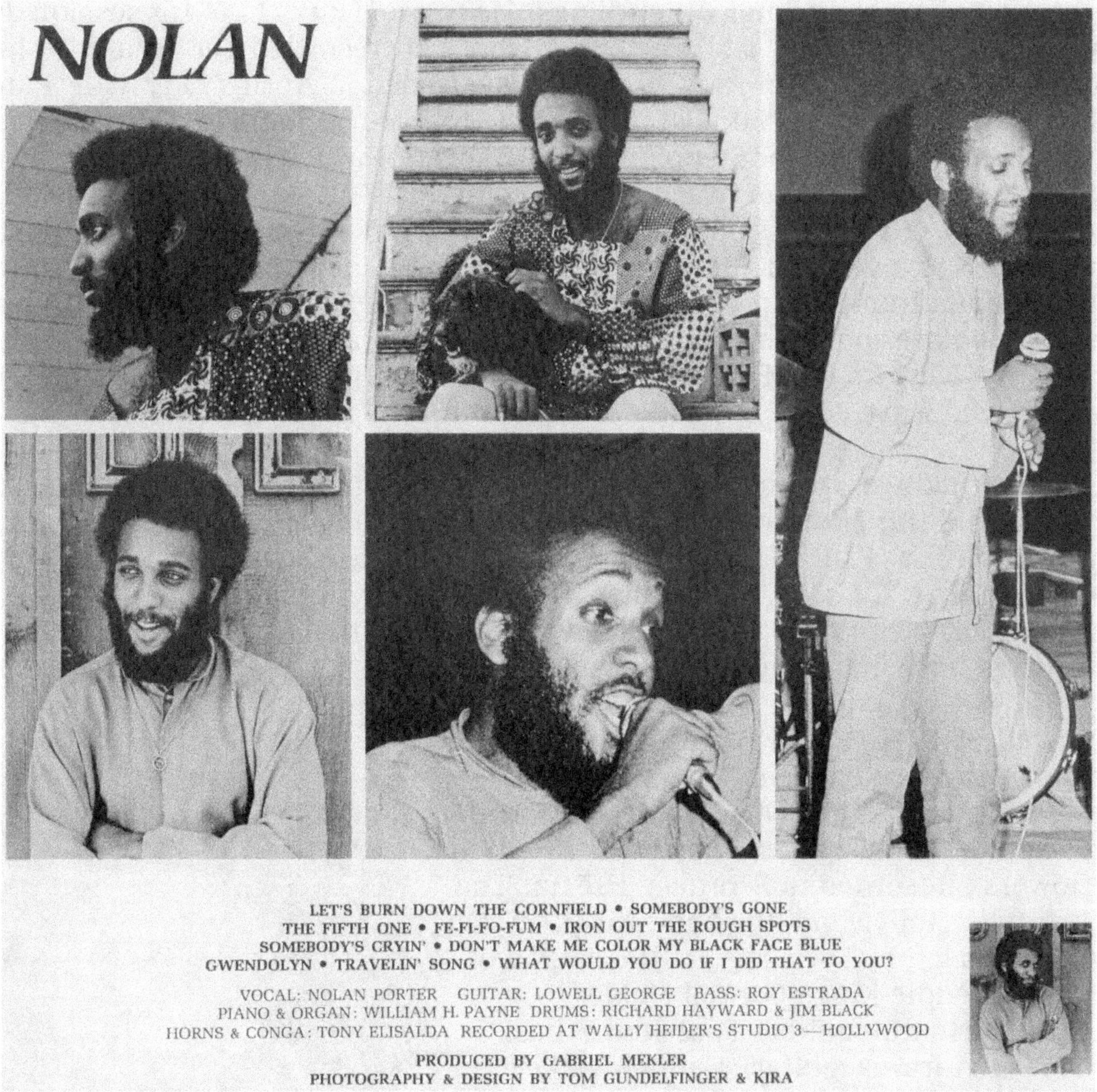

"Funky L.A." was an edited mono remix of the track on the LP below.

Regardless, Nolan was busy doing other things. He wrote "Funky L.A." for session drummer Paul Humphrey and his Cool Aid Chemists, who also recorded for Lizard. The album "Paul Humphrey And The Cool Aid Chemists" was issued in April 1971, with "Funky L.A." appearing two months later. "Funky L.A." was the follow-up single to "Cool Aid," a decent-sized hit for Humphrey and for Steppenwolf, the latter of which recorded the instrumental with new Mekler lyrics as "Move Over." Nolan Porter and Paul Humphrey sang "Funky L.A.," which covered the city's diverse population and lifestyles. It made a small splash on the R&B chart (#45) and a very small impression on the pop chart (one week at #109). "Funky L.A." got Porter and Humphrey on the June 5, 1971 episode of "American Bandstand," and it indicated that a more soul-influenced approach was the way for Nolan to go. Here's Nolan about the song: "I always felt 'Funky L.A.' had a haunting quality to it, that being that most of the people who leave come back, like 'Hotel California' in reverse."

Paul Humphrey had worked and/or recorded music ranging from easy listening to Frank Zappa. Nolan said this about recording with Humphrey: "I had never worked with another drummer as prolific as Paul. Whether Paul was recording for Michael Jackson or performing on Lawrence Welk's TV show, he always brought his own drumming genius and total understanding of what you wanted. He gave you beats that you hadn't thought of that made the songs have much hipper arrangements."

In the last half of 1970, Nolan Porter collaborated with drummer Richard Flowers. Together, they wrote the soul classic "Keep On Keeping On." The problem was that the song was mistakenly credited only to Flowers. Recorded in February 1971 at The Sound Factory in Hollywood, the band for "Keep On Keeping On" was led by Lee King, Jr., the cousin of guitar master Freddie King. Gabriel Mekler produced King (rhythm guitar), Paul Smith (bass), Richard Flowers (drums, guitar), George Walker (guitar), and The Blackberries on backing vocals.

Porter clearly remembered how "Keep On Keeping On" was created and what happened afterward: "Richard Flowers and I created the song together at a recording studio at Argyle Avenue and West Sunset Boulevard in Hollywood, California. Gabriel Mekler was preparing me for a tour and 'Keep On Keeping On' came as a surprise while jamming in the studio. Richard heard the saying 'Keep On Keeping On' when he was a child growing up in the south. It was a way of saying, 'be strong, don't give up.' I liked the expression and wrote the lyrics, keeping 'Keep On Keeping On' as the hook linking the verses. My lyrics described situations in which people might need strength and sustenance. Richard wrote the music line and established the rhythm. It was too bad that Lizard never gave me credit for writing the lyrics, and too bad I didn't call them on it. Lizard was breaking up while the song was becoming a hit, and I was very young and naive." Nolan performed "Keep On Keeping On" and "Crazy Love" on the January 15, 1972 episode of "Soul Train."

Right after "Keep On Keeping On" was laid down, a different set of musicians tracked "I Like

What You Give" (written by Porter and Mekler). Another of Nolan's most popular songs, "I Like What You Give" would be later covered by the likes of José Feliciano and Napoleon Murphy Brock (just prior to joining Frank Zappa's Mothers in 1973). Feliciano's version is on the 1974 album "For My Love...Mother Music," but Brock's version was never released. For this session, Mekler played organ and produced along with guitarist Mike Deasy, drummer Paul Humphrey, and bassist Ron Johnson. Johnson was the bass player in the Lizard group Salt 'N Pepper, which was led by the notorious Rick James. Salt 'N Pepper had recorded the album "Alice In Ghettoland" for Lizard, but it was not released. Nolan remembered that Rick James was involved in the pre-production for the song: "Rick James was rehearsing some of the material with me at Lizard Records during that time. Rick had a group called Salt 'N Pepper who was signed with Lizard and preparing to work on a show with me at The Troubadour. Ron Johnson was a big surprise. I thought he was an innovative bass player. Mike Deasy on guitar was a special treat because he was just as comfortable with R&B as rock, and his lead lines were musical poetry in either genre."

For "I Like What You Give," Nolan said: "When you listen to this song, you can hear the influence that reggae had on my voice. I tried to combine a lilting vocal with a crisp rhythmic lyric. It was my version of pop reggae. I was inspired in part by Johnny Nash, who later hit with "I Can See Clearly Now."

Just when things were starting to cook for Nolan Porter and Gabriel Mekler, Ampex stopped distributing the Lizard label at the end of February 1971. This abrupt change made the availability of Lizard's records a lot more difficult.

"I Like What You Give" and an edit of the year-old live version of "Somebody's Cryin'" formed the next Nolan single in late May 1971. Picked by Billboard magazine for the Soul Top 20, "I Like What You Give" only made #40 soul and #70 pop in separate 8-week runs. Sales were very slow for the first month, with the record appearing and then falling off both charts before returning again. Gabriel Mekler then began to release Nolan's 45s in different ways to get around the difficulties generated by the end of the Ampex partnership.

In mid-June 1971, the next order of business was to lay down "Groovin' (Out On Life)" at The Sound Factory in Hollywood. To complete this track, Mekler used previous contributors Clarence McDonald (keyboards), William Allen (bass) and

Paul Humphrey (drums) on the session along with guitarist Arthur Adams, sax player Charles Owens, Oscar Brashear (trumpet), female conga player Bobbie Porter (also no relation), and backing vocalist Abigail Haness. Nolan Porter recorded two different "Groovin'" lead vocals over the same finished backing track, and both were eventually released.

"Groovin' (Out On Life)" hit Nolan Porter's ears on vacation, as he recalled: "While Gabriel and I were in Montego Bay, Jamaica, we fell in love with the song. It was a hit in Jamaica and we thought it would be a hit in the US. Aretha Franklin had just come out with a song called "Rock Steady," which became a funky reggae hit in the States. After the reaction to "Rock Steady," Gabriel knew people would love reggae music in the US. So, we chose 'Groovin' (Out On Life)' to introduce reggae music to the American R&B market."

Meanwhile, Mekler had started up the offshoot label Vulture. This label was the home for Nolan's next single: "Groovin' (Out On Life)"/ "Gwendolyn." Unlike the previous releases, this single was released as by Frederick II. The A-side was listed without parentheses in its title, and the B-side was an edited mono remix of the "Nolan – No Apologies" album track. Issued in mid-September 1971, "Groovin' (Out On Life)" spent 10 weeks on the soul chart, reaching #25. It was Nolan Porter's largest soul hit.

Since neither "I Like What You Give" (as Nolan) and "Groovin' (Out On Life)" (as Frederick II) did the business they were expecting, Nolan and Gabriel Mekler released two tracks at the same time as "Groovin'" as by N.F. Porter: "Keep On Keeping On"/ "Don't Make Me Color My Black Face Blue." The A-side was in the can for seven months, while the B-side was a mono remix of the 16-month-old LP cut.

"Keep On Keeping On" was a moderate seller in the R&B market (a #39 sales peak), and it was also a small pop hit at #77. "Keep On Keeping On" has since become an in-demand tune on Britain's Northern Soul scene. In 1979, the British group Joy Division used the guitar riff from "Keep On Keeping On" as the basis for "Interzone" on their first album "Unknown Pleasures."

Billboard magazine connected all the dots and revealed in their September 18, 1971 issue that the records by Nolan, N.F. Porter and Frederick II were all by the same person - Nolan Porter! Apparently, Billboard was just as confused as the general public with these excellent records. That confusion would come to an end. Billboard also reported that Lizard was preparing Nolan's next album, and that it would be called "Nolan Frederick Porter II." That LP was never realized, but it would have included the singles tracks released after the first album. Concerning the name confusion, Nolan recalled: "Gabriel Mekler had some fantasy that he would show the American audience that these four artist names were all the same person on 'The Ed Sullivan Show.' He thought he would show just how clever we all were, but he was wrong!"

Frustrated by the experiences of his own label in the early summer of 1972, Gabriel Mekler made a deal with the ABC label to release Nolan Porter's records. It should be noted that Nolan Porter never signed with ABC and was never one of their artists. This was simply a deal in which Mekler licensed Nolan's previous Lizard/Vulture recordings and new Nolan Porter material to ABC. The licensing agreement was for one year, and both parties had the option to extend their agreement.

Here's Nolan about the arrangement: "I was not signed to ABC, but I had a friendly relationship with the VP of ABC Records. Gabriel was friends with ABC label president Jay Lasker, who signed him to the label as a producer. Again, I have to say I dropped the ball. All the brass at ABC liked me. They distributed my records and wanted me to hang out with them at the office. I didn't know how to schmooze and make small talk, and I kind of distanced myself from ABC. Also, I believe I was a bit gun shy from Gabriel and being screwed over by Lizard Records. I never held that against ABC."

Things got back on track in mid-August 1972. Working at The Sound Factory West in L.A., Gabriel Mekler obtained the highest rated L.A. session players to record with Nolan. Keyboardist Clarence McDonald was still on hand, accompanied by drummer Jim Gordon, bassist Ray Pohlman, guitarists Larry Carlton and Ron Elliott, sax player Charles Owens, trumpeter Oscar Brashear, and vocalists The Blackberries. The swinging R&B song "Baby" written by Nolan with Gordon Austin (but credited to Mekler and Austin without a mention of Nolan) was worked on for hours, eventually becoming "Baby Oh Baby" and finally "Oh Baby." Also cut at the same session was Mekler's catchy "Work It Out In The Morning."

While the results were strong, Nolan recalled that it was purely business: "These were strictly studio musicians. Gabriel gave them the formula and they delivered. I didn't have the same emotional connection with these musicians as I did with the earlier ones, like the guys from The Mothers and Little Feat. These players had a more commercial sound which helped me sell records, and for that I am grateful! Mekler had a knack for finding extremely talented guys, many of whom were well known at the time and some that would become very well known in the future, producing hits of their own."

Nolan continued: "'Oh Baby' addressed the feeling of loss when a lover is gone from their life, and the joy they feel when they return. This wasn't unusual, because I was frequently breaking up and getting back together with my girlfriends. I think also what prompted me to do the song was because I knew some of the musicians that would be playing on it and I wanted to give them a track they would enjoy."

Nolan completely connected with Mekler's "Work It Out In The Morning": "This was the way I thought lovers should resolve their issues. I felt that if lovers went to bed angry, they should certainly work things out in the morning."

The final session for ABC at The Sound Factory West came right afterward and was Nolan Porter's crowning achievement - "If I Could Only Be Sure" (written by Porter and Mekler) and the reggae/pop "Singer Man." Two different sets of musicians were required for the tracks, with only Gabriel Mekler and percussionist Tony Elisalda playing on both. On "If I Could Only Be Sure," Johnny "Guitar"

Watson played lead guitar, with rhythm guitarist Larry Carlton, drummer Jim Gordon and bassist Ray Pohlman forming the powerhouse rhythm section. "If I Could Only Be Sure" is considered Nolan's best recording and it has been reverently covered by the likes of Paul Weller (of The Jam and The Style Council) on his "Studio 150" album and similarly named live EP. The song's classic nature enabled Nolan to reach royalty status on the Northern Soul scene in England.

"Singer Man" featured bassist Wilton Felder and Paul Humphrey, and Nolan's treatment was much different than Three Dog Night's version a year later. This was Nolan's opinion of "Singer Man": "Gabriel knew I had a wide range of styles that I could mimic, but even though he appreciated the diversity in my voice, he was trying to find the best styles that best suited my voice. Gabriel and I had traveled to Jamaica together in 1971 and fell in love with reggae music, so he wanted me to learn a couple of reggae tunes that I liked while there. So, we chose 'Groovin' (Out On Life)' and 'Singer Man,' both of which were very popular while I was there in Jamaica. Three Dog Night put 'Singer Man' in a minor key and it did not work. I always felt it would have been a big hit for me in a major key."

Nolan put all of his experiences into "If I Could Only Be Sure": "At that time of my life, love and relationships weren't concrete or certain in my life. It was an expression of longing and loyalty to that longing. Johnny Watson's guitar expressed that longing."

An edited remix of "If I Could Only Be Sure" and "Work It Out In The Morning" were issued by ABC in mid-December 1972. Once again, sales were not what anyone was expecting. "If I Could Only Be Sure" spent eight weeks on the soul chart and made it up to #29, but pop sales were only enough to make it to #92. It was a criminal showing for a song now recognized as a major work.

Nolan Porter's ABC album "Nolan" was the first and only LP released under his own name and featured the new tracks along with stereo remixes of his Lizard and Vulture recordings. Other than "Let's Burn Down The Cornfield," the mixes of the older material were noticeably different than their original releases. "Groovin' (Out On Life)" had a different lead vocal track than the one released on the Vulture single, but the backing tracks were identical.

To generate additional interest in the album, ABC belatedly released "Singer Man"/"Oh Baby" in late May 1973. Neither the "Singer Man" single (which was remixed with an extra guitar track) nor the album performed well, and Mekler's work with Nolan and ABC ended quietly.

NOLAN

Below: Nolan was the centerpiece of the short-lived group A Touch Of Spice.

Nolan felt that it was time to leave the music scene for a while. He returned in 1978 and 1980 to record two sets of tracks with the sole purpose of attracting some attention. "Bird Without A Song" was the continuation of what Nolan laid down with "If I Could Only Be Sure," and he recorded versions of the song at both sessions. "Only A Thought Away" was a more pensive track, but just as strong as "Bird Without A Song." "It's Alright To Dream" found Nolan getting back into a smoother R&B groove. The other two tracks recorded in 1978 were completely unlike anything Nolan Porter had done until that point. "Cloudy" was a cover of the song that Paul Simon wrote with Bruce Woodley, while "City Lights" had Nolan going into Charley Pride country crossover territory. The lower register of Nolan's voice, as illustrated on Debra Piper's "City Lights," would be further explored as he got older.

About those demos, Nolan said: "In 1978, I recorded 'Only A Thought Away' and 'Bird Without A Song' at the Music Grinder recording studio (now closed) in West L.A. I met some excellent young musicians who were spiritual devotees of a young boy known as 'The 14-Year-Old Perfect Master' (born Prem Rawat) in India. Somehow, these musicians heard a very rough version of the songs with me playing piano. They originally believed they were recording it to become part of the theme music for an album introducing their teacher to the public! In 1980, Gordon Austin (co-writer of 'Oh Baby') and I went into a local recording studio to re-record some of my old songs for an agent just to get ourselves work around town. To our surprise, we liked some of our later arrangements better than the originals!"

Nolan and Gordon Austin.

"Actually, 'Bird Without A Song' was a comfortable blend of different styles, like classical and R&B. Since as a child my early training was in classical music and my musical training as a young adult was in rock and R&B, this song was a musical statement as a sign of me maturing, widening my horizons.

"I considered 'Only A Thought Away' classical soul. This song was co-written by my close friend and manager Sandra Cooper. This song helped me to process the passing of Gabriel Mekler in 1977. For 'It's Alright To Dream,' I dreamed of a house in the country, a white picket fence and one and a half children! It was definitely a fantasy on my part, but I still enjoyed the fantasy. Debra Piper wrote 'City Lights.' I wish I had written this song, and when I sang it I felt it was written for me. On 'Cloudy,' I tried to sing it in a jazz/R&B rhythmic style while maintaining the clarity of the story and lyric of the song."

When Gabriel Mekler passed away in a motorcycle accident on September 4, 1977, the entire Lizard/Vulture catalog was left unguarded. This has led to numerous unauthorized and/or unlicensed releases of Nolan Porter's material.

When Gordon Austin rejoined Nolan in 1980 to record some studio tracks, it was with the backing band Street Scene. Austin's song "Street Scene" was more like a modern "Funky L.A.," and "Every Little Move" was a sedate but effective number. The other three tracks were a surprisingly effective cover of The Doobie Brothers' "What A Fool Believes" (one of the few ever attempted) and re-recordings of "I Like What You Give" and "Oh Baby." Austin shared the vocal duties with Nolan.

About these sessions and reuniting with Austin, Nolan added: "Gordon Austin is a fine songwriter and friend. I thought he was one of the best ballad songwriters that I hung out with. Gordon and I used to harmonize a lot, and we recorded 'What A Fool Believes' purely for our own entertainment. 'Every Little Move' was one of Gordon's beautiful ballads. This song allowed me to croon like a loon!"

Nolan's friendship with Gordon Austin actually goes all the way back to their teenage years. Nolan and Gordon wrote three songs together that were copyrighted with the U.S. Library of Congress on September 11, 1967: "The Fountain Of Love," "When I Come Home," and "Why Do People Kill?". Although none of the three were officially recorded, these songs are clearly Nolan Porter's earliest original works.

Shades Of Gray

When nothing happened with the recordings made in 1978 and 1980, Nolan did not release anything for two decades. During the 1980s, he performed occasionally with his friend Timothy Nicely (né Paola) in the duo Shades Of Gray.

Nolan also had solo gigs in places like Singapore, Bali, and Alaska. Some of those were on cruise ships that Candy mentioned earlier. Porter's friend and manager Forrest Penner landed those cruise ship gigs for him.

During the vast majority of the 1980s and 1990s, Nolan Porter very quietly and carefully crafted his new performing persona. Whether playing live as a solo or in a duo, Nolan played many low-key, for-profit and charity gigs. If an organization needed a way to get their message out to the public, Nolan would get involved with the right people to create a musical work or themed show to reach the desired audience in a powerful way.

Songwriter Luanne Hunt collaborated with Nolan Porter on the musical "Dove Lessons." Its 1997 staging in Claremont, California raised more than $10,000 for the House Of Ruth shelter for domestic violence victims. Some of the original songs that were part of the framework of the musical were "Facets," "Vessel Of Light," "King And Queen Of Hollywood," and "Hard Work."

All of these photos are from Nolan's post-ABC period and show some of the many attributes of his performing career and personality.

In 1999, Nolan was asked by co-producer Jeffery Ward to do a cover of Screamin' Jay Hawkins' "I Put A Spell On You" for the film "The Quickie." It was recorded at GVS Studio in Van Nuys, California. After the film was first released in France on July 25, 2001, it went to DVD a couple of years later. Nolan's vocal on "I Put A Spell On You" is so surprising that you can't believe it's him, but it is!

Let's hear what Nolan thought of "I Put A Spell On You": "I was honored when Jeffery Ward asked me to do this song for the film 'The Quickie.' It allowed me to stretch my acting and musical ability in ways that I had not foreseen. It's the closest I've ever come to channeling Screamin' Jay Hawkins!"

Nolan Porter had met Patrice "Candy" Zappa around the time of "I Put A Spell On You," and as we know, they found that their voices worked very well together. Their first recording session together was the aforementioned Brian Hudson And The Popular Front CD "Condoleeza Condoleeza" in 2004. About the Hudson experience, Nolan said this: "Brian Hudson is a very talented singer/songwriter/attorney that I started working with in the late '90s. Brian's original material was very topical and sometimes political. We put on a few shows between 2002 and 2005, with a definite political slant. These shows rang true with the audience and were a good showcase for my voice and Patrice's voice."

This was followed up by recordings with my group Neonfire in 2005. The Neonfire tracks were highlighted by the Nolan/Candy duet "Alive" and Nolan's emotive vocal on "Lying Down." Here are some final comments from Nolan: "Patrice Zappa and I started singing together in 1999, and 'Alive,' written and produced by Greg Russo, was about as good a song as could have been written to showcase our singing talents together. 'Lying Down' allowed me to drop down and sing in my lower register, which I enjoyed immensely. This song was an old story to a new and cool beat. Well done, Greg!"

Candy has pointed out that circumstances changed dramatically in early 2006 after she received an email from someone in Wales inquiring if Nolan was alive. As we know, Candy and Nolan packed their bags, and Nolan went down a storm in Wales and Manchester, England. The Manchester trip forged a solid relationship with Harry and Diana Grundy, presenters of the soul-based radio program "The Right Track." Northern Soul fans were extremely enthusiastic, as were other DJs throughout the UK that

 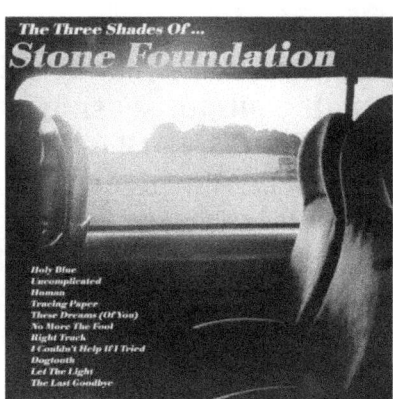 

played this type of classic music. Nolan's popularity spiked upward, eventually leading to his meeting with the Midlands-based band Stone Foundation. They would become his official British backing group starting in 2010.

Nolan Porter recorded the songs "Tracing Paper" and "Right Track" with Stone Foundation for their 2010 CD "Away From The Grain," and both tracks were repeated on the following year's compilation "The Three Shades Of...Stone Foundation." "Tracing Paper" was also a single A-side in early 2011.

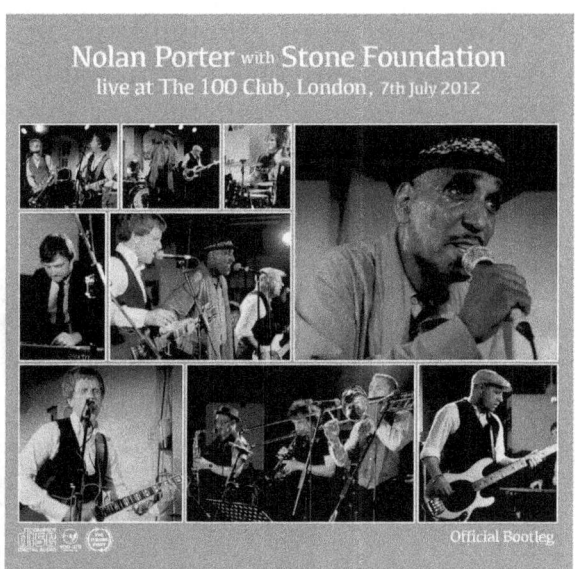

Their July 2012 joint UK tour was a smash and led to the limited-edition CD "Live At The 100 Club" released on August 24, 2012. The 100 Club CD was drawn from their gig on July 7, and only 500 copies of the CD were manufactured. In addition to the very spirited performances, another notable aspect of the album is that it was not presented in super high fidelity. In fact, it was recorded as if you were in the audience. That is precisely why the album was noted as an "official bootleg" on its front cover. The CD is now a prized collector's item.

Nolan's re-recording of "Fe-Fi-Fo-Fum" with Stone Foundation was released as a single in early 2013, and their redo of "Crazy Love" was included on the Stone Foundation CD "Finding The Spirit" in 2014. During the album sessions, they also recorded a new version of "The Fifth One," but it has not been released. "Finding The Spirit" also featured Nolan's backing vocals on the song "Bring Back The Happiness." The band's friend Lee Cogswell had been filming how Nolan and Stone Foundation worked together live and in the studio, and Cogswell's documentary "Keep On Keepin' On" first aired in the UK on June 22, 2013. That short film became part of Stone Foundation's DVD "To Find The Spirit." BBC Birmingham and BBC Radio 6 Music sessions in August 2014 reached new fans for both Nolan and Stone Foundation. The Birmingham session featured just Stone Foundation guitarist Neil Jones with Nolan, while the Radio 6 segment included the entire band.

Nolan Porter and Patrice "Candy" Zappa's music catalogs made their digital debuts in July 2011. Both of Nolan's albums were also released on CD in 2014.

Yet another career highlight for Nolan Porter took place on October 8, 2015 at the Fonda Theatre in Los Angeles, when Nolan shared the stage with Paul Weller to perform "Heat Wave" during Weller's second encore. Photographer Charles Gonzalez was on hand to document the proceedings.

The non-Stone Foundation releases on this page summarize the frustration that fans have been dealing with concerning Nolan Porter's recordings.

Above left: the Record Store Day release of "Keep On Keeping On"/ "If I Could Only Be Sure." The A-side was taken from a record, while the tape used for the B-side had digital distortion. Also, Nolan was supposed to be credited for co-writing "Keep On Keeping On" with Richard Flowers. On the label of this record, Flowers is the only name listed. For these reasons, it's definitely a must to avoid.

The Light Of Love Wax Co. and Outta Sight 45s (below left and right, respectively) correctly credit Nolan Porter and Richard Flowers for "Keep On Keeping On." Light Of Love, founded by vocalist Gloria Jones, has been issuing Northern Soul favorites for charity. Stone Foundation's "Beverley," with Nolan's backing vocals, was yet another release in their growing catalog.

The Outta Sight 45 honored Nolan's role in the Blackpool Soul Festival in 2018. Thanks to Charles Gonzalez for the photos on the next two pages!

The final Nolan Porter and Stone Foundation studio collaboration was "Beverley" on the 2015 CD "A Life Unlimited." Nolan provided backing vocals on the song. "Beverley" was also released as a Light Of Love Wax Co. single in early 2016. Competing single reissues of "Keep On Keeping On"/ "If I Could Only Be Sure" were respectively issued in the Netherlands by ABC/Universal (a 2005 Record Store Day limited edition release of 1,000 copies), a UK issue in 2006 by Light Of Love Wax Co., and another British issue, this time by the Outta Sight label in 2018. The Outta Sight single was a commemorative issue to celebrate Nolan's appearance at the Blackpool Soul Festival that took place between June 15-17, 2018. Nolan closed out the first day of the festival.

The final original Nolan Porter release was the single "Go-Go-Go" in late 2017. It was issued by the Soulside Productions label in the US. Nolan wrote the lyrics for "Go-Go-Go," and Candy provided backing vocals. As usual, Nolan was not credited for his compositional efforts, but the producers made sure their names were prominently displayed. Some things never change.

The Northern Soul band The Signatures became Nolan's last backing band during a two-week tour of England and Mallorca in October 2019. As fans in the final section of this book will attest, Nolan was at the top of his game.

Nolan's last interaction with Stone Foundation was during the online "Stone Foundation & Friends" streaming webcast on June 10, 2020. With Neil Jones on guitar, Nolan sang "If I Could Only Be Sure." It was a fitting way for Nolan to deal with the COVID pandemic and reconnect with his fans.

BEHIND THE SCENES

Nolan always liked parties. If you gave him a glass of chardonnay, he would do anything at a party for you. This are just some of the very many occasions where Nolan and I went to a party and Nolan's friend Forrest Penner photographed what went on.

"Sure, I'll put on a dress!" You can just imagine what I thought about this display! With chardonnay in hand, Nolan was ready for a good time.
From left to right, Nolan is with Sarah Cooper (daughter of his friend Daniel Cooper) and Sasha Casey.
At the top of the next page is Nolan with Cooper's son David.

77

Susan Skinner is on the left of both the top photo here and the bottom photo on the previous page. Between Susan and Nolan are Jay Skinner and his wife Kate Hudson. Maria Herbst is at the left of the bottom photo.

This page highlights Nolan's interactions with his co-workers at Westside Regional Center.

At right: nothing beats a lunch out with the crew!

(l. to r.): Nolan with José Reyes and Antonio Gonzalez. Incidentally, both José and Antonio are in the picture above. See if you can spot them!

Nolan with Antonio Gonzalez during a break from a holiday party.

FRIENDS AND FAMILY REMEMBER NOLAN PORTER

ANTONIO GONZALEZ (photos on page 81):
I still can't believe he is gone. It seems like not too long ago we were going to lunch together. I met Nolan when I started working at Westside Regional Center in November 2006. He was working in the mailroom. He was such as a nice, unassuming guy when I met him. I remember seeing him at our company picnic with a tape recorder and earphones practicing songs for an upcoming performance he had. That's when I knew he was a professional singer.

In November 2007, I went to a doo-wop convention in Las Vegas and saw a book on Northern Soul. I looked at it and saw that it had a page on Nolan. I had to get it for him. When I went back to work, I gave him the book. He was so appreciative. He talked about his gigs in Europe and performing with different people. I had always hoped to one day be able to accompany him to Europe. I told Nolan that there was a Northern Soul scene in L.A. and we would go check out different places. Nolan met some people that had his records and they took pictures with him.

In 2010, he had this idea to have a fundraiser for The Achievable Foundation. He wanted us to sing oldies like in the song "Memories of El Monte" (co-written by Frank Zappa). I had never sung in front of audience before, but Nolan encouraged me to do it. I remember harmonizing and practicing some doo-wop songs with José Reyes and Nolan during our breaks at work. I will never forget that night where we performed at the Santa Monica Elks with Candy Zappa, Nolan, José and Danny Delgadillo singing those classic oldies like "Blue Moon" and "Pretty Little Angel Eyes."

As the years went on, we would go to lunch together at least once or twice a month. We would talk about music as well as what life was like for him in the 1960s and 1970s. Nolan was always a positive guy. He was very encouraging and always looked at the brighter side of things. Whenever they asked him to sing at work for different events, he would always oblige. Over the years, whenever he had a gig with his wife Candy, I would always try and make it. I always wanted to be supportive of Nolan just as he was supportive of me. Nolan was a giant of a man with a big heart. He was a great friend. I loved him and miss him.

"DR. DOT" (DOROTHY STEIN) (photo on page 36):
I was in L.A. for a TV project and was happy that Patrice and Nolan had some free time to meet me at my hotel to shoot the breeze, have a drink and some laughs with me (this was June 2015). I have always had a soft spot in my heart for Patrice; she is one of my favorite people on earth. This was my first time meeting Nolan and I got to see why she was so in love with this man. He was very polite, kind and genuine. He accented Patrice's conversation with me. I loved how he wasn't overbearing like some husbands can be. He was the perfect gentleman, and I absolutely loved his sense of humor. We all met again when they came to the east coast and visited me in Jersey City; thinking that was about a year later; the spring of 2016. We all walked over to a great little pub/restaurant near me called the Fox & Crow. Nolan helped Patrice walk, as her back was keeping her in pain. I LOVED how he tended to her and took care of her. They were pleased to be seated in the sort of speakeasy back room where they had jazz concerts. You wouldn't know it by

walking by it. You would think it's just an average bar with some tables that served food. However, as we passed through the sort of secret door into the back, Nolan and Patrice were excited and grinning ear to ear – like they were in their element. I quietly told the bar owner who they were, and he was beaming with pride to have them both there as guests. I am pretty sure they got a couple free beverages and were also announced from the band on stage - sort of a "hello" shout-out. We dined and watched the jazz artists play and had a helluva time. I could tell that Nolan was itching to get up and sing (most artists DO want to go up and join in), so that was sweet to observe. I WISHED they had called him up, but you know how it goes. I was sad to see them depart as that was the last time I saw Nolan. However, pretty much each time I called Patrice to chat (usually once a month; sometimes more), Nolan was always chiming in with laughter and sometimes jokes. Patrice would sometimes pass the phone to him and we would chat too. Only after his passing and my podcast I did with Patrice did I dive deep into his music and WOW! I am amazed at the music he has left for us to enjoy. I didn't realize what a legend he was until he was gone. He didn't behave like a star, but he certainly IS one and he will shine on forever. I simply LOVED how incredibly happy he made Patrice.

ANDREW CALARA:
I played bass for Nolan during his L.A.-area shows for about 5-6 years. Honestly, I loved playing the shows, but I loved the practices and just hanging out even more. It was sort of like hanging out with my rock 'n roll grandpa. He always took me under his wing. I remember how he and Patrice would roll up to practice with pizza or orange chicken. No one I ever worked with under 40 ever did that for me! Free beer is good, and free pizza is even better!

Nolan and Patrice would just shoot the shit with us for most of a practice...talking about old stories about Johnny "Guitar" Watson and Rick James and whoever. We'd book a three-hour practice, and honestly, we'd actually practice music maybe half of that time. I like that Nolan trusted us to learn the parts like pros, and we usually did. I remember how he'd take me aside after a good practice and tell me that "wow, you are a really great bass player" or "wow, you have a really good singing voice...you should sing more!" I don't think I've ever had anyone encourage me or believe in me more musically than Nolan did.

What I remember most is that one time we were hanging after practice and Nolan started talking about encountering a California condor on a college campus back in the '70s or '80s. And me, being a naturalist, knew that there were only 20 or 30 California condors still alive at that time, and I thought to myself, there ain't no fucking way he saw one! And I was like, "Nolan, you sure it wasn't a hawk or a vulture? There aren't that many condors left out there!" He turned to me and insisted that he saw a California condor, and I had no choice but to believe in him, cause that's what he did - Nolan Porter made you believe.

DAVID GLASBAND:
I was a runaway at 17 years old in 1970, with a bench warrant for my arrest, staying with Nolan in L.A. at 3320 Descanso Drive, where he allowed me to stay where I felt safe. I wrote my first song, "Los Angeles," while sitting on the balcony overlooking downtown L.A. at Nolan's apartment in one day. It was a smoggy day (that's part of the lyrics). I was an innocent, young teenager scared to death of being caught one more time after running away from the 5th juvenile court placement and Synanon. I used to wear a harmonica holder like Bob Dylan and played a blues part which accompanied the guitar part of my song.

I sat with Nolan that morning and told him that I was going to Minnesota. I was scared of pursuing my music career because of the number of people one degree removed from me dropping dead from drug overdoses: Janis Joplin, Jim Morrison, Jimi Hendrix, etc. I knew I was way too immature to survive.

I got to witness firsthand and up close to what happened to Nolan, getting ripped off by the attorney for Lizard Records. Lizard's office on the Sunset Strip was where I also got to meet Gabriel Mekler, Nolan's producer who discovered Janis Joplin and who produced the group Steppenwolf, Nolan, and other famous recording artists. The attorney used his legal knowledge to run away with all of Gabriel and Nolan's money. Nolan never got over the impact of the betrayal he experienced from that unfortunate episode. Gabriel died shortly thereafter, so Nolan was on his own.

Nolan suffered and struggled severely in his life from that experience, but he never became bitter. That is a testament to Nolan's inner spirit and strength he possessed inherent to his persona and character.

FERN BLOOM:
Nolan learned that my son Philip was an aspiring musician. So, every time he'd see him, he'd come and talk to him and just "shoot the breeze" by asking him what he was up to. He was always genuinely interested in his music and business path. I remember SO many times after Philip's car accident and many months of hospital stays, when Nolan would come and ask us how he's doing to give inspiration on healing. It meant a lot of how thoughtful he was.

When we were doing a Purim play at temple many years ago, I brought funny hats for the cast to wear and to be silly. Nolan played the king and brought fun, singing and joy to a higher level for all. It was just great!

Nolan was always so thoughtful and caring. He would be the schlepper to help everyone in need. No one had to ask for help - he just stepped right in. What a mensch! Always with a GREAT BIG SMILE and a BIG HEART.

His voice would make everyone listen in awe. Ross and I had the additional pleasure of going up a concert with Patrice and Nolan performing. We couldn't stop smiling and dancing along during the show. A GREAT team and talent. Love you both!

SAM WARD (TREACHEROUS CRETINS):
In July 2019, I was fortunate enough to meet Nolan and Candy at the Zappanale Festival in Bad Doberan, Germany. I was playing there with my band Treacherous Cretins, and we had invited Candy up to sing "Uncle Remus" with us. It was a hit! Nolan and Candy watched our whole set from the side of the stage, and they were so supportive and encouraging. It was an honor for us to have them behind us. On the following Monday morning, after the festival had finished and most of the festival-goers had already started to make their way home, I was walking through the Kamp in the center of Bad Doberan. To my delight, I ran into Nolan again. We shook hands and chatted for a couple of minutes. He was once again so supportive, paying compliments to me and the band, giving me advice about life and music, and warmly encouraging me never to give up! I only met Nolan that weekend, and did not know him well, but I will treasure the memory of our conversation forever and always remember his warm, genuinely kind nature. He is sorely missed.

BRIAN HUDSON:
Nolan Porter was an irrepressibly generous, spirit-lifting, life-loving sunny fucking day. So decent and open-hearted, so far removed from the grudge work and suspicions and ugly chatter that runs through most of us, he seemed simply to be some kind of new and improved human being, incapable of rancor toward anyone but greedy music execs. I saw him angry just once—but it wasn't volatile anger, it was a kind of John Lewis anger, outraged and correct, and driven to undo a familial injustice. His brother had denied him access to his elderly mother. I offered him some legal advice, and he persisted until he had his day in court. As I recall, relations with his mother were never rectified. It gnawed at him, I think. And that was that.

Twenty-some years before that, he convinced me to perform in public songs I had written, that I'd sometimes have him sing, just to hear what his voice could make of them. And that voice had the richness and seductive gravity that sinks deep, with a resonance like Nat King Cole—and could've rebuilt "The House That Nat Built," if Capitol Records had had the smarts to put a mic in front of him, though management surely would have frowned on Nolan's gorgeous take on "Condoleezza," based on Nat's "Mona Lisa." Nonetheless, our "Nat" doing my snarky political stuff was heaven for me.

Indeed, I remember Nolan and Patrice and Lee Boek and my wife Joan backing me like a heavenly choir on a song I had written about the cardinal of Los Angeles having recently erected a shiny new $200,000,000 church, while neck deep in pedophile cover-ups. My obliging choir lifted their arms in solemn piety on the chorus, "It's Cardinal Mahoney's... erection!"

The last time I saw him perform, he and Patrice and a tight quintet played at a club in Hollywood, maybe forty or so attending. Despite the small turnout, Nolan delivered, R&B and funk, bluesy, grainy, belting it out. And Patrice blew the roof off with her cathedral voice (a true Zappa) and damn near rocked herself off her chair. I was touched by the open affection he showed her, while they were working, overflowing on the stage.

The last time I talked to him he had been ill for many months. It was right after the 2020 election, and though we had deep political differences, we resolved them with good will and good faith, and with what, even a grudge-working, suspicious, chatter brain like me, can only describe as love. I miss him terribly—and feel for Patrice in the terrible chasm she now inhabits, absent her irreplaceable Nolan. His kind of love affair with the world is just too goddamn rare; we're lucky we had the fruitful years he gave us. Goodbye, Nolan Porter.

NEIL SHEASBY (STONE FOUNDATION) (photos on pages 26-32):
At the turn of 2012, we were on somewhat of a collective comedown. That's what music and creativity does to you; for every high a low. Our band Stone Foundation had recently experienced what the view looked like from the top of a peak, at the back end of the previous year (2011) we'd been invited to support ska legends The Specials on their extensive tour of the UK where we performed in huge arenas to approximately 8,000 people most nights. It was an incredible opportunity but one for which we fully prepared for. It catapulted our name and reputation to a higher trajectory, and it also resulted in attracting more of an audience to our own gigs and events. We swiftly followed up on it by touring on our steam off the back of this. Then suddenly when that action ceased, we were left with a sinking feeling of deflation, wondering what next? How do we maintain creative momentum?

Thankfully the phone rang and it all became clear...a couple of years previous, back in 2010, we'd been approached by a promoter on the Northern Soul scene who was bringing over artists from the United States to do public appearances at regional club nights as part of the fledgling underground soul circuit here in the UK. The deal with these type of engagements is that the artist normally performs four or five of their most well-known songs at a Northern Soul night in between various DJ sets. Usually, it's not uncommon for them to sing over a pre-recorded backing track. Thankfully, this particular promoter was keen to find a live band to back his latest pending arrival from the States.

We got the call. I'd have probably have been skeptical in most circumstances. We were also planning on beginning our next album and due to start recording, but the one thing that swayed us was the artist that we were being asked to work with: Nolan Porter.

I'd first heard Nolan's music via the mod scene back in the early '80s, his tune "Keep On Keeping On" was a dance floor anthem. "If I Could Only Be Sure" was also a favorite, one that was a highly sought after record for the young modernist, which was only heightened a decade or so later when Paul Weller covered the song for his "Studio 150" album. So, I had full knowledge and an appreciation of who Nolan Porter was, and we were not going to turn down this opportunity.

Right from the get-go, we hit it off with Nolan, musically, creatively, and personally. The whole collaboration just clicked immediately. Naturally, we'd done our homework and learned almost everything from his two albums "Nolan" and "Nolan - No Apologies" even if on this occasion we would only be playing a cut down set with him. We really gelled with him and both parties were keen to continue what we had begun. We vowed to make it happen again, but not via a third party promoter calling the shots. So, that's what transpired...

That summer of 2012, it was we ourselves, Stone Foundation, that financed and funded the flights to get Nolan back over to England, where this time around we'd booked not only full gig dates but a tour itinerary that included some festival engagements. We wanted to do things properly on our own terms - no half measures.

We also planned to utilize some time to record together plus our friend and filmmaker Lee Cogswell was on hand to document everything and capture our time together on camera. It was during this time that our connection blossomed. This went way beyond music and we cemented a deep bond with Nolan as a person. We really got to know him as a man and his influence and inspiration upon us took hold. He was of course a generation apart from myself and Neil Jones in years, but that became no barrier to our enduring friendship. In fact, we looked up to Nolan as someone we could learn from both in his craft, and more importantly, as a person.

He had a calming presence, an aura, a light, complete positivity. He'd been through a lot, had his fingers burned by the music industry but he never once regaled us with hard luck stories or any hint of bitterness. It was part of the learning process and the journey to Nolan, and he appeared grateful for having been granted the opportunity to express his art in the first place.

When he came to the UK, it was obviously apparent that he was knocked out by the love and appreciation for his music over here. I think he was fairly amazed and fascinated by the fact that so many people possessed such a knowledge and understanding of his music. He was humbled and genuinely moved by that.

We soon gained his trust too. He realized that we weren't trying to make money from our work together. We'd break even and pay Nolan as respectfully as possible of course, but the bigger picture here was creating something that is left behind forever, like a time capsule to be discovered whenever that may be - a future legacy. Therefore, both myself, Neil and Nolan were keen to write something new as well as visit his former glories of the past. We had a couple of ideas, songs such as "Tracing Paper," "Right track" and "Bring Back The Happiness," all of which heavily featured Nolan's vocals.

We re-recorded a couple of things from Nolan's back catalogue, such as "Fe-Fi-Fo-Fum" and also spent a spectacular evening putting down an incredible interpretation of the Van Morrison song "Crazy Love" that was one of those unique and unrepeatable moments that you very seldomly stumble upon as musicians. It was magical and something that stays with you and never forget. It's like lightning in a bottle.

As our touring schedule unfolded and took us further afield to play festivals in Spain, I would room with Nolan on the odd occasion, and I'd get to know him even more. For all of his undeniable charisma and magnetic presence on stage (which of course you need to front a band), he was a gentle soul, intelligent, humorous, engaging and gracious. He was always as interested in you than talking about himself.

One thing that was evident that really chimed with me was just how much love he radiated towards his relationship with his wife Patrice. His eyes lit up when he spoke of her and it was obvious he missed her whilst away from home and wanted her to experience everything he was whilst over here. I could totally identify with that, also being grateful and thankful for having been blessed with the love of a family that I adore. We'd go out for dinner too whilst having downtime from gigging and recording, Neil's family, our friend Scott, my wife Claire and my kids, Neil's grandad Mick...

Nolan became part of our extended Stone Foundation family. He had time and conversation for everyone. We loved the man. It went way beyond just a musical bond. That was just our initial common ground that connected us.

Sometimes in this old life you get lucky and circumstance guides you to certain situations and people. Some folk drift in and out of your life or sail through it. Others remain a permanent fixture on your memory. They are the ones that make a difference, no matter how big or small - the sort you can learn from and be inspired by, the ones you aspire to be a little bit more like, to take a leaf out of their book, the ones that make you a better person, the ones that can evaporate negativity from your conversation and provoke positive thinking, the ones that light up a room, the ones that make you belly laugh, the ones that are not only interesting but interested, the ones you learn to love.

These are the ones that you miss the most. Nolan Porter was all of these things and more. I'm blessed that we could call him our friend.

ROBERT WIGLEY:
England was a very different place in the 1970s: political turmoil, mired in national debt and wildcat strikes by the workforce throughout the country. There were frequent "rotating" power cuts which would leave your household plunged into darkness for several hours without warning, and in the winter, without heat. There was a three-day week, which left workers short of money, and high taxation, which made the rich leave the country in droves. In short, it was a mess.

This was the backcloth to my teenage years. I lived in a small mining village in the north of England. Add to this raging hormones, a strong feeling of "being different" and wanting to break away from the normal life which was laid out for many at that time: a cycle of school, mining coal, marriage, kids and death!

For me, my "escape" was to be music; the BBC spoon-fed the teenage population via national Radio One. Glam Rock was the buzz word, Progressive Rock was the long-haired student's choice, and Donny Osmond made all the pubescent girls swoon with his crooning of "Puppy Love." I didn't fit in with any of the above.

I had two older sisters who had grown up and bought records in the golden era of the 1960s. They had both married young and left home, leaving their records behind. I began to play through these abandoned 45s and soon found I liked the sound from America: Stax, Atlantic and Tamla Motown, with their driving beats and lyrical genius. Roy "C"'s "Shotgun Wedding" was a particular favorite. Although I didn't quite understand the message in the song, I loved its soul vibe.

At the age of 14, I stumbled across a small youth club in a nearby town. I remember walking through the doors and hearing a mighty sound of heavy guitar riffs and drumbeats. The dance floor was heaving with dancers all moving to this pounding beat. I could hear the singer wailing "We got to keep on, keeping on." This was my first introduction to Nolan Porter aka N. F. Porter! The next day, I went to the record store to try and buy this record and no one knew it!

I was soon drawn into an underground scene, a network of clubs playing 1960s and '70s American Soul music that wasn't mainstream. DJs would hunt down records that had been neglected in the States and bring them to the UK to become huge and sought after records here. The rarer the records, the higher the price became.

I started buying these obscure records and discovered "Oh Baby" on the ABC label — could N. F. Porter also be Nolan Porter? He sounded the same, but the records were totally different. My searching soon uncovered two albums, with more songs and indeed a picture of Nolan along with the incredible "If I Could Only Be Sure" a dead cert dance floor winner. But as these records were cutouts cheaply imported into the UK and already several years old, there was no real information to exactly who Nolan Porter was, or indeed if he was still alive, recording or making music.

In those days, there was no Internet, Google searching or instant fix for information. The records were the life blood of an underground movement and Nolan "N. F." Porter was a star of that scene.

Fast forward 30 years and it's a different world. I'd been lucky, travelling to the USA frequently, searching out and buying records and still totally hooked on the music. I had a "day job" driving freight trains full of coal, but I also had become a DJ and a promoter on the underground scene I discovered as a teenager. This scene had led me to meeting many of my heroes and indeed becoming friends with dozens of American soul singers and musicians. Because of this, I was asked to become part of a new promotion team for Pontins at one of their holiday centers in Prestatyn, North Wales. We conceived an event, a full weekend of soul music featuring DJs and a showcase of live acts made up of artists flown in from America specifically to sing their songs which were hits on this underground scene.

The internet had exploded in the mid-1990s, and clips on YouTube of the Northern Soul scene had been seen by artists in the USA, including Nolan Porter. We had several people working on contacting or trying to find artists for our showcases including myself, Rob Thomas and Bernie O'Brien. Finally, contact was made and in March 2006, Nolan was heading to the UK to perform his hits to a 4,000-strong appreciative crowd.

As MC on the showcase, I got to meet the artists on a more personal level. Nolan had brought along his partner and soulmate Patrice and they had extended their stay for a few days after the show, basing themselves in Manchester. Now, Manchester is a great place, but not exactly the best tourist or cultural hot spot in the UK. I asked them if they liked Robin Hood, as I lived near Sherwood Forest, and arranged to pick them up a few days after the show. They both travelled over to Sheffield on the train from Manchester and I took them into Robin Hood country, visiting Edwinstowe and The Major Oak, where legend has it Robin Hood used to hide from the Sheriff of Nottingham in this ancient hollow tree.

They came to my home in Worksop and we went for a meal locally before heading back that evening for the train to Manchester. Nolan and Patrice were very friendly and humble, but I was on Cloud 9. This working class boy had just spent a whole day with one of my heroes whose record I'd first heard as a 14-year-old boy. I showed Nolan some of the records in my collection, including a Brazilian 45 release of "If I Could Only Be Sure" on Probe Records. He was totally unaware of this release!

We kept in touch, and when Nolan came back to Manchester to perform at Chris and Marcelle Waterman's Ratcliff All-Nighter on the 28th July 2012. My future wife Claire and I were there to see him, going backstage to spend some quality time catching up with this lovely man in person once again. The thing about Nolan was his brilliant smile, as soon as he saw us, his face lit up and that smile beamed out. I remember hugging him as he went through, having just come off stage and knocking the crowd dead! He may not have received the recognition or monetary rewards in his home country, but his performances in the UK showed what a mighty talent he possessed. He clearly loved every minute.

As a result of these shows, Nolan became involved with West Midlands based DJ Hitsville Chalky, who hooked him up with local Midlands band Stone Foundation, who I also knew as we moved in the same circles. This resulted in Nolan coming back to the UK to record and tour with the band in the Summer of 2014, including a gig at the iconic 100 Club venue on Oxford Street in London on the 24th July – nearly two years to the day that I'd last seen him.

Although living 150 miles away, I travelled down to London on the train for the mid-week gig to meet Nolan again. I went into the infamous dressing room where the greats in music history from The Rolling Stones, Sex Pistols to Amy Winehouse have waited to go on stage. As I walked through the door, I was immediately met with that great man's smile; Nolan was always the same, a lovely genuine guy. Needless to say, Stone Foundation and Nolan had the capacity crowd yelling for more. After the encore I said my goodbyes and grabbed a selfie with Nolan before heading back north on the midnight train. Little did I know that that would be the last time I would see Nolan alive. In recent years, we kept in touch via Facebook and phone calls and Patrice would always ask my advice if Nolan was approached to do gigs in Europe to weed out any unscrupulous promoters.

I am pleased and honored to have known him and to have spent quality time with Nolan and Patrice, both in person and via other means of communication. Make no mistake, Nolan was a huge star in the UK and Europe and was taken from us far too young. I treasure his recordings and still feature them in my DJ sets. Nolan, you made a working class kid very happy with your music and shone a bright light into my life in dark times. I am proud to have met you and called you a genuine friend.

ANGEL TEJEDA (THE MUDD CLUB MÉXICO - ZAPPA FAN CLUB FOUNDER):
For a guy like me, having been born in Mexico and being an indisputable member of Generation X, it has not been easy to be neither in the place nor at the time that I would have liked, especially when most of the music that I love was made during the '60s and '70s in Europe and the United States. Already in my 40s, life has been very generous with me. I must have done something good, first to deserve the trust of Patrice Zappa Porter and then to have the privilege of sharing friendship with her.

Thanks to this, I had the opportunity to meet Nolan Porter the same day that I met Patrice. My surprise was very great when I discovered the kind of gentleman that he was, a super-friendly man, attentive, affectionate, always ready to talk about any subject, and interested in what I was talking to him about at all times. He was an extraordinary man who had great talent, had an excellent voice and an incredible rhythm, but above all else, Nolan was a loving man who was filled with love and took care of Patrice until the last moment of his life.

His departure has been a great loss for music and especially for his family, and those of us who have had the privilege of having known him, I send you all my affection and admiration wherever you are, dear Nolan.

MICHAEL ROTH:
My friendship with Nolan began in our senior year in high school, at L.A. High School. During the 10th and 11th grade, Nolan was at Newbury Park Academy in Thousand Oaks. I believe it was kind of a boarding school. At L.A. High, there was a group of us who were involved in theater arts and music who were all a pretty wide group of people who tended to hang out together a lot, the artsy crowd. I was very involved in theater, and when the music department did productions, I would help out on stage crew. My two best friends throughout high school were Roger Hickey, my best male friend, who was more involved in art but also participated in stage crew, and Rochelle King (now Rochelle Flynn) who was also involved in theater. Rochelle at that point was Roger's girlfriend, and so the three of us hung out a lot.

I don't specifically remember "meeting" Nolan, but he began hanging out with us. Like all groups of friends, we sort of had our own way of interacting, our own styles, our own kind of dialogs, our own humor, and Nolan seemed to instantly get it and fit in with us. When I called Rochelle to inform her that Nolan was dying and we began reminiscing a bit about him, I made the statement that "I don't remember meeting him, it was just like all of a sudden in our senior year he was there and it was as if he was always there" and Rochelle said, "Yes, yes, that's exactly the way it was." It was like we'd always known each other, and he found his group at L.A. High kind of effortlessly. He just sort of slid into it as though he was always there. I don't know if it was that effortless but my impression was he felt very at home at L.A. High.

I should mention perhaps that the school was predominantly black and I'm sure that was not the case at Newbury Park Academy. Although, I think of Nolan as being very multi-cultural and certainly not one to be defined by his ethnicity because he was broader and more universal than that. Nonetheless, my impression was at the time that it was probably very comforting to him to be around a largely African-American community. And definitely there was a "crowd" of us that were very involved in the arts, particularly music and theater, and he definitely fit in really well with this larger circle of people.

I think it might have been the previous year that I went to the Shrine Auditorium to see this rock band called The Mothers of Invention led by some strange guy named Frank Zappa. Of course, nothing ever became of them and I'm sure you never heard of them! I went with a few friends, but I don't specifically recall Nolan being there. He'd probably have mentioned it if he was.

Nolan became involved in musical productions at L.A. High School. The music teacher and director of those productions was a man named Bill Roderick. Bill liked Nolan a lot. Anyway, also involved in those musical productions was a girl named Liz who became my girlfriend during our senior year. One of their products was selected scenes from "Porgy And Bess," and Nolan and Liz were the two lead singers. I clearly recall Nolan singing "It Ain't Necessarily So" which he sang really well.

Nolan did some theater as well. We were involved in a Shakespeare Festival which involved putting together like a 30- or 40-minute composite of a certain Shakespeare play. We did scenes from "Othello." I can't recall if all the participants did Othello, or if we just chose it. I think it was that everybody was doing Othello and the fact that Nolan was black and Othello was black (often played by the likes of Lawrence Olivier in blackface). Anyway, Nolan played Othello terrifically, and a good friend of ours named Richard Stolarz played Iago. I was in it as well, and I was very involved in choosing and editing our segment. A good friend of ours named James Farrell who had moved from L.A High to Van Nuys High that year was our chief competition. James was a terrific actor. He was a great friend to us both. James also played Othello and another friend of James's played Iago. One of us won and the other got second place, and I am not sure whether we were No. 1 or No. 2, but I recall it was a fantastic experience. It was done at UCLA's Royce Hall, and it was a thrill for us youngsters to perform on that stage. It was a pretty full audience as I recall, as they were obviously friends and family of all the actors from a couple of dozen schools that participated.

At that time, some major life-changing issues were going on around us that certainly affected our views of the world. The civil rights movement was tremendously relevant to our lives at a multi-racial school such as L.A. High. Also of great impact to us all was the Vietnam

War, which we were beginning to pay serious attention to as it escalated. No matter how you viewed the war, it was going to have a direct impact on your life in those days, and I would say our generation was unique in the history of the US. At that point, failure to register for the draft was a federal offense punishable by up to five years in prison. So as young men, we had to make up our minds about the draft and the war, and we were the first generation to massively refuse to go. Nolan and I both registered ultimately when we turned 18. I ended up applying for conscientious objector status, which I was denied. I'm not sure ultimately how Nolan got out of going. We each had friends from L.A. High who went to Vietnam and were killed over there. I remember Nolan and I discussing Mohammed Ali's refusal to fight in Vietnam while his right to sit and eat in a restaurant of his choosing was denied in his own country. We were mesmerized at the site of Ali saying on TV, "No Vietnamese ever called me a nigger!"

For much of our senior year, both Nolan and I worked at Orbach's department store. It was on Wilshire Boulevardlvd, just east of the May Co. at Wilshire and Fairfax, and it was between the May Co. and the L.A. County Art Museum. Nolan and I worked for a couple of hours in the evening in the employee kitchen, running the dishwashing equipment and a few other tasks. We often sang while we worked. Especially, I remember us singing "Rollin' and Tumblin,'" a classic blues standard, which we'd learned from Canned Heat, a hot blues band in L.A. at that time who became pretty well known nationally. Nolan and I had both seen them perform in L.A. at local clubs - a superb blues band. Then after the kitchen, we both put on our nice clothes and went out in the floor as salesmen. I worked in the men's clothing department, but I don't recall what department Nolan worked in. I remember a couple of the women in the kitchen always laughed because when Nolan and I arrived at work, we'd always shake hands, even though we saw each other almost every night and also went to school together. It was more like giving each other five than a formal handshake most likely, but still they got a laugh out of it.

Anyway, one had to make a choice – you'll go if called or you'll refuse. At that point, the possibility of a prison sentence was serious, so you really had to make some serious decisions. We were all just beginning to learn about the war and question it. I recall Nolan, Roger and I and a few others having serious late-night discussions about it. We had a wonderful art teacher named Stu Allingham, a young guy for a teacher, well, he was about 30, but I remember we had numerous chats with him, sometimes at the Carnation coffee shop near my house, about the war and other things about growing up and he was very supportive to us all. I remember him telling us "Don't you dare go to that awful war," and he said he'd do anything to support us all to avoid it.

Roger and I were probably the principal culprits who introduced Nolan to marijuana, getting him started on something he would enjoy throughout his life. After high school, Roger, Nolan and I moved out of our parents' homes into our first apartment on Edgecliff St. in Silverlake for $60 a month. The landlord didn't like us and thought we were hippies, which we were. We had our mattresses on the floor, and I don't know if we had any furniture to speak of. He would always say to us, "You're just camping out in there!" Nolan and I went to L.A. City College and Roger went to Otis Art Institute on a scholarship, which he squandered. I don't recall ever studying much in those days. When the landlord eventually kicked us out after a few months, we went around the house. It was I think just a one bedroom apartment, but we took all the doors off their hinges, unscrewed them, and put the doors onto the roof. With chalk or something like that we scrawled on the big bathroom mirror, "When the revolution comes, the landlords will be the first to go!"

At that time, the hippie "movement" was in full flowering, and during our senior year and the following year, Nolan and I and probably Roger hitchhiked up to the Bay Area more than once, staying at the home of a friend of ours. Later, like a year after high school, I moved up to Berkeley and lived in a small house behind a black Baptist church in West Berkeley where every Sunday morning we'd hear the congregation rocking and rolling as black churches do. The minister of the church and a few of the church elders were very nice to us, with one of them referring to us as "you crazy hippie white boys, you need to come to church and come to Jesus with us," although obviously we weren't all white.

After that first apartment on Edgecliff, we all moved into this duplex off of Echo Park Ave. where a friend of ours named Herb had a couple of barrels of pot that he sold bags from. A good bit of LSD was consumed from time to time, and I remember Nolan and I participating in a couple of crazy evenings taking acid with other folks, although the details are sketchy about what occurred during those crazy evenings. No orgies or any of those stereotypical visions people have of the '60s, but a lot of partying, loud music and various drugs. I mentioned the Berkeley scene, and Nolan loved going up to Berkeley. Once we arrived there, Nolan got out and kissed the ground, calling Berkeley the "city of love." It was a bit of an exaggeration, but it was a pretty cool place in those days, quite the hotbed of hippieness and left-wing political activism.

Opposition to the Vietnam War was huge in those days, and Nolan and I participated in quite a few marches. Once at a "Free Huey Newton" rally, organized by the Black Panther Party, after chairman Bobby Seale got the crowd pretty whipped up, we were all chanting "Free Huey, Free Huey" when the cops began tear-gassing the crowd and swinging their batons around. I think I got hit in the back by one of their night sticks, all the while coughing and my eyes stinging terribly from the tear gas. Nolan got quite a dose of tear gas as well. I lost track of him in the confusion, but later we found each other and made our way back to the rear of the church. We had a similar experience in L.A. at an anti-war rally once.

For most of the '70s I lived away from L.A. On one of my visits back, I recall going to the art gallery at Barnsdale Park in East Hollywood with Nolan. Afterwards, we were walking down Sunset Boulevard beside the park when coming in the opposite direction was a hippie type, long-haired guy who was walking down the street stark naked, greeting us with a friendly hello, acting like it was the most normal thing in the world. Nolan always recalled that event thusly: "Me and Michael were walking down the street talking about God when this hippie guy walked by us stark naked." I don't recall specifically that we were "talking about God" but I do remember the naked guy walking past us like it was totally normal.

Sometime during 1969 I'd say, I was back in L.A. from the Bay Area, when our good friend J. Douglas Halford contacted Nolan, Roger and I insisting that we come up to San Francisco for a "revolutionary meeting of the greatest importance." J. Douglas, or Jay as we called him, was a poet-playwright-aspiring screenwriter and ex-convict, not necessarily in any order and a very close friend of us all since we became friends in Echo Park. Jay at that time was working with the Seventh Step Foundation, which helped get ex-cons situated after serving their sentences, and Jay was sponsoring a sort of black revolutionary mystic named Raymond Scott. The meeting in San Francisco was to celebrate Raymond's release from prison and the formation of some sort of revolutionary alliance. There were 12 of us at that meeting and there were references to another historical meeting of 12 disciples about 2,000 years previous. I remember that we all sat in a circle, there was a bowl of joints in the middle, and we talked all night. Much of the conversation had to do with the Vietnam War and its increasing escalation. Shortly thereafter I returned to Berkeley and got involved in a group helping to ferret draft-dodgers up to the Vancouver area in Canada. I was involved in a few such trips. I don't think Nolan was ever directly involved with that, but he was around at times. Anyway, that "group of 12" never formally met again like that, but I did have some contacts with a few of those folks.

I recall that to get to that meeting, Nolan, Roger and I decided to go down to the rail yards east of downtown L.A. to try to hop a freight up to Oakland. We were chased off by the rail yard guards and their guard dogs. They threatened us with severe bodily harm if they ever saw any of us again, and as I recall the way they looked and acted, they were not joking. We never tried to hop a freight again. Fortunately, hitchhiking was pretty easy in those days and we managed to make our way to the Bay Area in time for this important gathering.

To catch a ride in those days you'd stand at a freeway on-ramp with a sign that said what your destination was. I must have gone back and forth between L.A. and the Bay Area two or three dozen times and it was rarely difficult. It's amazing to think about it now.

In L.A. around that time, as well as in San Francisco and Berkeley, there were "love-ins" and "be-ins" where crowds would gather in Griffith or Elysian Park in L.A., Golden Gate Park in San Francisco, and People's Park in Berkeley. Crowds would gather and rock music acts would perform. I recall being with Nolan at several of those events, seeing such bands as Jefferson Airplane, The Grateful Dead, Big Brother & the Holding Company (fronted by Janis Joplin), Country Joe & The Fish. All of them were Bay Area bands. In L.A., particularly popular at such events were The Doors, the blues band Canned Heat, and The Chambers Brothers, whose signature song "Time Has Come Today" was a huge hit at those events. Country Joe's anti-war anthem "I Feel Like I'm Fixin' To Die" was also a big hit. I recall seeing such anti-war luminaries as Angela Davis of the Black Panther party, poet Allen Ginsberg, noted LSD advocate Timothy Leary and others, often with Nolan.

I have a distinct memory of going in a car loaded on acid down to Huntington Beach to see The Paul Butterfield Blues Band (God knows who was driving and what state of inebriation he was in). We were also in a similar state going to see the legendary Cream at either the Fillmore or Avalon Ballroom in the Haight-Ashbury District where we all hung out frequently in San Francisco during that era.

LESLIE BAKER:
My friendship with Nolan Porter began decades ago as I was just starting to have a music career playing bass. Nolan was a great singer with wonderful musicianship. He was truly kind, fair and generous. We got along great and had many opportunities to work together. One in particular stands out when we played the House Of Blues on the Sunset Strip. Not

every gig was on as grand a stage as that. By that time, Patrice was with us.

I knew Nolan before he met Patrice Zappa. I remember the phone call when Nolan excitedly told me he had met the most wonderful person - Patrice Zappa! He let me know she's Frank Zappa's sister and she can really sing. He wanted me to meet her, and I did. Nolan's love for her seemed very strong - they had found the loves of their lives, blended their voices and sometimes performed together. Nolan liked me to write music charts for him to take to his jobs in England and Europe where musicians there would play for him. One day, Nolan and Patrice came by my place to get a plan together for some new charts. They brought loads of Chinese takeout food with them, which was great. We had a really fun afternoon with laughs, dogs and music. Nolan let me know later that the charts worked perfect for his English band.

We, Nolan's circle of friends, were all sad and concerned when Nolan became seriously ill. Patrice allowed and encouraged me and my husband Joe to visit him, and we did. On that last visit, I sang him my newest original song. I didn't think I had the voice to pull it off, yet Nolan said I sang beautifully. Now that he's gone and I look back on it, I realize Nolan was a rock - he was rock steady with his smile, his positivity, and his ability to deliver for his audience. Can you understand how his encouragement, good vibes and the respect he had for me gave me strength to keep myself together when difficult situations came up? That's a reason to call him a very important and dearly loved friend. I certainly miss him. Those of us who knew Nolan Porter can continue to draw strength from the memory of his kindness. If you didn't get to know him, we're hoping this collection of remembrances will give you a glimpse and a smile.

ART AND TERESA UTNEHMER (photo of Art on page 12):
Nolan was one of those individuals that could really light you up. It was like you touched metal after getting some kinetic energy. You would feel a pop. He gave off that kind of energy. He had an honest interest in people and would make you feel really good about yourself and whatever you were doing. You would feel like you were lifted up, like you had been enlightened. I remember seeing him perform in L.A. and it was magic. We will absolutely miss him and his wonderful smile and voice.

BRYAN FOX (DJ):
Thanks to Marv Mac, I had the thrill of being on the dance floor for one of Nolan's last performances as well as the privilege of meeting and talking with him. It is a time I will treasure always — for multiple reasons, not the least of which was to learn how much it meant to him to share HIS soul with others. It was always a joy to spin Nolan's music and to watch it received in the dance floor. I will always treasure the chance to meet him and talk and enjoy the live groove. HEY!! You are a treasure and a solid legend, Nolan!

JOYCE GRANVILLE:
I met Nolan Porter in around 1979. He lived in a little apartment complex in Silver Lake, California. He was friends with a friend who lived there too. A guy who was a documentary film director, who's name may have been Ron? Ron did a documentary on Nolan and filmed it, and I interviewed Nolan on the film. Nolan sang some songs too. He was very good and a delightful person. I was sorry to hear he has passed away this year. Rest in peace,

Nolan. You were special!

KIRK MacLACHLAN:
Sending my condolences to your family. Sharing fond memories of the late '60s when I played congas with Nolan. I always appreciated his warm support and kind encouragement.

JOHN SMITH:
My heartfelt sympathy to Patrice, his family, and his friends. Bless you all. Nolan had wider musical tastes than some of you might know. He was a key member of our madrigal group. We mainly sang Elizabethan and special occasion songs - not quite the same kind of music he wrote or sang on tour. He was one of the friendliest, nicest, humorous, and willing people I have ever met. The coronavirus kept us from meeting for most of a year. It was a shock to learn of his illness. It seemed not very long after that I heard the stunning news of his passing. He was a great soul and will be sorely missed. Rest in peace, my friend.

Here's the madrigal group featuring Nolan Porter and John Smith (left). Nolan took this group very seriously and performed those ornate songs with gusto!

ANJANETTE ROBINSON:
Nolan, I will miss you dearly. You are such an amazing friend with a beautiful smile! And your eyes (you know we have had so many conversations about your resemblance to my father). I will forever cherish all of our conversations, and all that I have learned from you about music and travels. I am sending wishes and prayers for Patrice and your family. May you rest in the peace, greatness, and honor that you deserve! Love ya my friend, and may God watch over you!!!!

SORYL MARKOWITZ:
Nolan was a very special soul. Our dear, dear friend. He was a talented musician, kind and compassionate and loving man who cared deeply for others. He brought joy and humor to our lives. He was part of our family, Michael's oldest friend, our son's godfather and my colleague all wrapped up in one beautiful being. Our heartfelt condolences to Patrice and Julie. Rest In Peace, dear Nolan. We miss you already.

FELICE GARDNER:
My deepest condolences to sweet Nolan, his beloved wife and all of those that love and miss him. I worked with Nolan at WRC for the last 8.5 years and he honestly was the epitome of a RAY of sunshine. I never passed him in the halls at WRC or chatted with him in the lunchroom without seeing him smile and give some, if not many, positive words of wisdom. He was one of a kind, and we were all gifted with knowing him and calling him a friend. He'll be missed but NEVER forgotten. I know all of us that know him will keep a little piece of us with him. When we find ourselves complaining or being negative, hopefully we'll ask ourselves, "What would Nolan say?" and hopefully an answer of peace and happiness will come to us. Rest In Peace, sweet Nolan

IMELDA PALACIOS:
♥

EREIDA GALDA:
May your beautiful soul Rest In Peace...thank you for all the years of support to our staff and families. You never made us feel we were bothering you, no matter how last-minute or spontaneous our boardroom changes were. We were blessed with your kind heart, bright smile and music. My condolences to your family. You will be missed, dear Nolan.

SANDY CABANATAN:
It broke my heart to hear the news that such an amazing co-worker passed away. I can't imagine going back to work without hearing Nolan's morning greetings or hearing a tale from his younger days in between coffee breaks or even having the chance to watch Nolan perform. My heartfelt condolences to Nolan's family and to everyone who was impacted by this amazing man. He will never be forgotten.

FEBEN FANTU:
May God rest Nolan in peace and give his loved ones the strength to endure this painful loss. I will forever remember your genuine kindness and your bright smile.

MERIL PLATZER:
Nolan, you are loved and your spirit, wide smile, and great music will live on. ♥ Luv Meril

TERESA KELLER:
I feel blessed to have worked with Nolan. His kindness was shared with everyone he met. He helped me when I was injured, and his thoughtfulness really made a difference. May he rest in peace.

DARLENE MAIRO:
Oh Nolan...you will be so missed...your smile, your caring energy and your very special way of communicating, be it through the spoken word or your music....you were always present.... Really present....My heartfelt condolences to your family and friends....you are so loved....RIP

MEGAN MENDES:
Deepest condolences to Nolan's closest friends and family for this loss. Nolan was a wonderful person who I had the pleasure of getting to know over the past six years of my working at Westside Regional Center. I loved talking with him about music and seeing him perform! He took special interest in my husband's work within the Syrian refugee community and always asked what he was up to. Such a thoughtful person! He will be missed!

COREY LEE CONROY:
To the family and friends of Nolan Porter, I am deeply saddened to learn that Nolan has passed on. I'll never forget his big warm smile and open nature. We used to talk in the break room about life. Nolan was hard-working and always willing to help. He is already deeply missed. I know he went on in to heaven where he is living it up. I pray for your peace and comfort during this difficult time. Keep on keeping on, Nolan. Save a place for all of us.

STANCEY DeLUCA:
There are so many personal "stop and talk moments" shared over the years at Westside with Nolan. The joy he exuded simply being present with you: he was attentive, engaged, sensitive and always kind. He had the most wonderful laugh that would erupt in conversations, always bringing a lingering brightness, a gentle deep and curious soul. His life was well lived and well loved.

THE SIGNATURES (photos on pages 42, 44 and 45):
The whole band are totally heartbroken to hear of the passing of Nolan Porter. We had such an amazing time on our two-week tour with Nolan in 2019. The whole band totally enjoyed every minute of the tour by spending time with the beautiful soul of Nolan Porter - a dream fulfilled for some members. Three dates in the UK and then across to Mallorca, we had a blast and made memories to last a lifetime. You had the most beautiful soul and will be missed but never forgotten. In 2020, we should have seen Nolan return to the UK for some more dates across the UK and Ireland with us. COVID prevented that, and sadly it will now never be. The stories, the fun, the walks along the beach in Mallorca and the MUSIC will always hold a special memory for us all. Rest in Peace, Nolan Porter. Thank you for the memories.

CANDACE HEIN:
Nolan seemed to be everywhere in the regional center - always doing his job, yet helping anyone who asked. WRC was fortunate to have such a talented, funny, wise, friendly and down-to-earth soul in our midst. I miss his smile already.

MARTHA THOMPSON:
A wonderful and kind man...Nolan you will be missed.

WANDA LEAVEY:
I will always remember Nolan's warmth, fantastic smile and great talent! Wishing all his family peace in their hearts.

ANDREA AND KEITH JONES:
Through our son Neil, we had the great pleasure of meeting Nolan and seeing him perform live during his stay with us. We knew we were in the presence of an exceptional person. He was a very kind and caring soul who loved his wife and family immensely. I can't believe he is gone as we had so hoped to catch up with him again, but we're happy in the memories he gave us during his stay in our home.

PAUL MOONEY:
Rest, Nolan.

STUART BULL:
RIP Nolan. Thank you for the great music. God Bless. KTF

GRISELDA GOVEA:
♥

NANCY FADER:
I'm so happy I knew you, Nolan.

VALERIE LATTANZA:
I was lucky enough to know Nolan for 30 years or so, first through dear friends and then through work. I am sure he would have had no idea how many people he influenced and how beloved he was. My son saw him as a mentor and inspiration in all things musical, and my daughter knew him as very wise and kind. I feel like when Nolan and I would chat it often went deep very quickly, or I learned a random, interesting and new fact about his life, there was always one! I will miss you, dear man. Condolences to his beloved Patrice.

AGA SPATZIER:
RIP Dear Nolan, my birthday buddy. You shared so much kindness and joy with us. WRC will not be the same without you.

GAIL SMITH:
Nolan was a dear WRC friend. He charmed and entertained us with beautiful song and always had a warm smile and cheerful greeting for whomever he encountered at work. Very sorry for your loss.

CARMINE MANICONE:
Nolan will be missed by many people - always positive, thoughtful with a good listening ear. He was a mensch! God Bless you Nolan - my condolences to Patrice and your family.

SIMON JOSEPHS (at right with Nolan at The 100 Club):
♥

JOHN GREENHALGH:
He was very kind to my father-in-law. A very charitable man.

PHYLLIS ROSECRANS:
I met Nolan in the early '70s when he was living with my friend Susan. How lucky can one get – music, joy, and laughter! I loved Nolan from the start, and he always had a big heart for everyone! We lived in Silverlake on Descanso. They lived upstairs and I lived downstairs under them. I remember I grew a big plant outside my apartment on the side of the hill. When I would go down the hill to check on it, I would notice buds missing. I knew Nolan must have been down there. Ha ha! We had a lot of high times. His talent was extraordinary and yet he was always humble and encouraged me in my own talents. I would sing along with him just for fun and it seemed like it was just a celebration every day. Many years later working at Canter's and Assoc., Nolan and I were on a sales team selling educational programs to teachers and schools all over the USA. We had a lot of success helping teachers with discipline management in the classroom (what classrooms now!!?). I remember going to see Nolan sing in the choir at his temple on a holiday. Everyone looked pretty contained, but Nolan was a singing it down with soul!!! That's Nolan - full of soul. I will always love him and miss him as he really touched my soul!!!!!

DAWN DRANGLE (photo on page 14):
I remember meeting Nolan when he and Patrice were first dating, and thinking "wow, what a real genuinely sweet man!" Immediately, I knew that he and she were perfect for each other. Nolan was true to his character at all times. He always had a kind word and an inclusive demeanor. I remember him even telling me once, after hearing me sing karaoke, that I should do something with my voice (I never did). I so miss the days when he and Patrice would come visit me at the beach in Carpinteria or when I would drive down to L.A. to catch one of their shows or celebrate a birthday. Just hanging out was a real treat.

What I will miss the most about Nolan was his unwavering love and dedication to his wife Patrice. It meant so much to me that my dear friend Patrice of so many years had found her soulmate and the love of her life. Nolan, I will miss your smile and your friendship and your warmth, my dear friend. Rest in the arms of the Lord. We will meet again, although not too soon.

JULIE WATERMAN (photos on pages 14, 36, 45 and 47):
I loved Nolan dearly for being the first man to love and respect my mother the way a good man should.

PATTY McGILLAVRY:
I met Nolan and Patrice for the first time when they made the trip from L.A. to Ottawa,

Ontario for a special fundraising concert. They arrived late at night and I was asked to greet them. We had a late dinner together and we talked into the wee hours of the night. It was the beginning of a wonderful friendship. The concert the next night was sold out, and we all had a wonderful night.

Nolan was so talented and dynamic on stage. He had the gift of being able to draw in the audience and make them feel like a part of the show. You couldn't sit at one of his performances, because within the first few minutes, the entire audience would be on their feet, dancing all night long. He was so charismatic.

I will always remember Nolan as a true gentleman. He always called me "Miss Patty" with a special kind and caring tone in his voice, which always filled my heart with warmth and love. He cared about people, and it showed. He is deeply missed by all, but his musical legacy will live on forever.

BEN PEGLEY (THE SIGNATURES):

A beautiful soul was lost today. I had the consummate honor and privilege to be his guitar sideman for a small UK tour in late 2019, and an amazing, long weekend abroad in Mallorca and another live show. There are so many ways in which I could (and often do) wax lyrical about my brief time as his guitar sideman, but I can sum it up in one instance after the show in Mallorca.

The venue was a good mile or so from the hotel where we were all staying, so of course there was a car laid on to take Nolan back after the show. I remember the first thing Nolan did when he was offered that ride was turn to us in the band and say, "What are you guys gonna do?" We said that we were gonna walk, maybe see if there was some food on the way. He said that he'd like to hang with us and walk too. So that's what we did. We all went together and walked and talked and got some food and just had a great time.

That was Nolan. He was the star, but he preferred to hang with us and just be one of the guys. I can't tell you how cool that was, and how rare. Before leaving Mallorca he gave me a parting gift of a Frank Zappa t-shirt. We had talked about Frank quite a bit on several occasions of course, and that tee was amazing!

I have been fortunate enough to have met and worked with many great artists in a sideman capacity and it's almost always a pleasure and an honor. But it isn't often too much more than that, and that's OK. With Nolan, right from the first rehearsal, he was instantly just the greatest, loveliest gentleman. We bonded over a kebab somewhere in northern England, talked Zappa and a hundred other things until far too late, and played his wonderful music to hundreds of adoring soulies. We played, we talked, we laughed, and he got deep in all our hearts. I will miss him terribly and my heart breaks for his family. Thank you Nolan, forever in my heart you are. You were incredible.

MARI LINVILLE (photographer of Shades Of Gray):
Nolan and his friend Timothy Nicely were loaned a house in the Hollywood Hills to shoot their short comedy film about Beethoven's half brother, Brohoven, played by Nolan. The house was amazing. It was filled with antique furnishing and musical instruments. Timothy talked Nolan into wearing pink tights and an Afro wig spray painted white. Nolan was such a good sport. The outfit was hilarious!

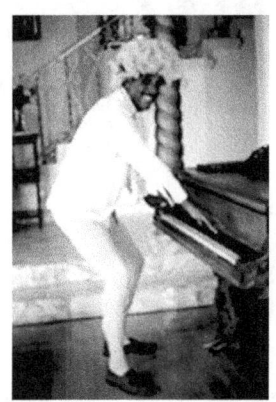

CARLO DIDCOTT AND SUE:
What a wonderful man. We met Nolan Porter at a gig in Melton Mowbray, Leicestershire England, performing with The Signatures. Nolan performed with such energy and enthusiasm. We particularly enjoyed "If I Could Only Be Sure" and "Keep On Keeping On." We were also thrilled to met him after the performance and found him a friendly, gracious gentleman with a great sense of humor. He asked questions about us and was interested to hear we came from Nottinghamshire, home of Robin Hood. Nolan was greatly amused when we told him that when we visited America we used to tell people that we were distant relations of Robin Hood - not true of course. We found Nolan to be down to earth, a warm person and wonderful singer and entertainer. We felt very privileged to meet him and cherish this memory. Love, Carlo and Sue xx

JOE MARCANGELO:
Big love. Nolan was taken in by the Northern Soul scene and is well respected/loved. Also, the amazing Neil Jones and his band Stone Foundation got work with him. For me, what they did was special.

ESMOND MORGAN:
Nolan is still played at Northern Soul gigs across Britain every weekend (normally). We will never forget him, and we will keep him in our hearts.

GALE CLINE:
He was a wonderful, generous and compassionate man for as long as I have known him...

which was way back in the day when he was in high school...hang in there, Patrice, you were a gift to him as he was to you!

JOSÉ RENDON:
The last few weeks have been incredibly difficult. A few days ago, on Thursday, February 4th at about 8:15 PM, right before I went to his house, I got word from his wife Patrice Zappa-Porter that my big brother, my mentor, mi carnal, a very good friend...mi hermano, Nolan Frederick Porter, had passed away. He was someone I admired and loved very much. I am so grateful for the opportunity I had to be a part of his life, to play music with him - something we were both so passionate about...and to have been able to spend time with him during his last few weeks with us.

Nolan was family to me. I had the privilege of being his drummer for most local (Los Angeles-area) gigs the last 8-9 years. We had so many plans to go back in the studio to write and work on new material. Nolan really wanted to get together and rehearse. We had plans to record and we were working on a tour to Mexico. Nolan was so supportive. Wow.

So many things I am going to miss about Nolan: his phone calls, his warm embrace...he would say, "Hey José" with a big smile...I am really going to miss playing shows with him, going out to dinner and just talking about life. I am definitely going to miss celebrating our birthdays together (I was born on May 9th and Nolan on May 10th). Nolan had so much talent and an amazing voice. I could go on for days...

FORREST PENNER:
With deep sadness, our dear friend Nolan Frederick Porter, passed away Thursday from liver cancer. One of the nicest and talented people I have known. I was fortunate to have collaborated with him writing and recording songs. I managed him for a short time in the '80s, getting him bookings on cruise ships. Nolan lived in our Echo Park guest house for 13 years and moved out when he met the love of his life, Patrice Zappa-Porter. Our life was so rich for having known him. He was so loving, generous in spirit and kind. So many memories, so many Xmas Eve parties where he sat at the keyboard and sang Xmas songs. Maria and I will have you in our hearts always. RIP my friend.

LUANNE HUNT:
LOSING A FRIEND AND AN R&B LEGEND. RIP to my cherished friend Nolan Porter, one of the sweetest, and most talented men on earth. My heart goes out to his lovely wife, Patrice Zappa, who Nolan loved more than life itself. This journey here is so hard at times. Thankfully we have one another to lean on in our darkest hours.

Nolan was a very popular R&B star in Europe in the 1970s, and his records are still in high demand to this day. Twenty-some years ago, I had the pleasure of being in a little duo with him for a short time and it's an experience I will never forget. We also collaborated on a musical about domestic violence, which raised over $10,000 in one performance for the cause.

HALI BURTON:
Nolan has been on my mind, and I realized I had not seen him recently on Facebook. I came here to read this horrible news. My friendship with Nolan started in 1967, when we did a summer theatre program run by the L.A. Parks & Recreation. In 1977, I was hired as a singer/actor by TAPLA, the Theatre Arts Program of Los Angeles. How wonderful it was that Nolan was also a new hire. We loved reconnecting, and a couple years later, we formed a cover band to play casuals. We would run into each other over the years. In the 1990s-2000s, I took my parents to High Holy Day services at Creative Arts Temple. How amazing to see my dear friend Nolan in the choir! I looked forward each year to seeing him again, and to have a chat. In 2015, a friend of mine was doing Menotti's "The Unicorn, The Gorgon And The Manticore," which is one of the pieces we sang in 1967. Nolan met me there, and we had a wonderful afternoon reminiscing. That was the last time I saw him. My heart is breaking for you, for me, and for all who loved this lovely and talented man. Just wanted to add my heartfelt condolences on this crushing loss. I love you, Nolan.

By Michelle Mills
For Dabelly Magazine

Luanne Hunt and Nolan Porter Steam Up the Coffee Gallery

Tucked away just before the hills in Altadena, Calif. is a little club inside a coffee house aptly dubbed ,The Coffee Gallery Backstage. I traveled out to this neat place to check out a delightful duo- Luanne Hunt, an Ontario area vocal coach, and Nolan Porter, a top musician from the '70s.

The lights dimmed and the keyboard tinkled with some jazzy pop sounds and Porter rolled out a couple of well-done covers, then Hunt warmly welcomed the crowd to the show. Hunt writes about life experiences and shares bits and pieces of stories in between the tunes, weaving a pleasant web to draw the audience closer until they change from fans to friends.

Their first tune, "Facets," recognizes the circle of life. It is bittersweet, but very positive and thought-provoking and the duo's harmonies were a treat to the ears. They went on to present "Vessel of Light," a song written about a part of Vincent Van Gogh's life which is usually ignored, the time he spent as a pastor. The tune is very folksy and tells a good story.

Hunt and Porter also gave the crowd a few tunes from their musical on domestic violence, which recently served as a fund-raiser for the House of Ruth. Hunt showed her talent for acting and employed props to set the stage for the songs. She also has a terrific sense of comedy. Hunt traded quips with Porter and gave some spicy commentary on her partner's musical abilities to the crowd.

Porter took his moment too with a great little number, "King and Queen of Hollywood," about a homeless couple who always try to look their best when they stroll the streets. He also gave the audience a great jazz tune, "Hard Work," which perked everyone up.

If you need a mellow evening in a relaxed atmosphere, you should look up Hunt and Porter. They not only make beautiful music together, they have style!

CHRISTOPHER GARCIA (THE GRANDMOTHERS OF INVENTION):
Mr. Nolan Porter: one of the kindest, most gentle souls I have had the privilege of meeting and getting to know over the years. You could be in the middle of a hurricane and standing next to him and he would say, "oh...it's raining" – not because he wasn't scared or excited. I believe it was because he didn't react to situations – he responded to them. If someone was acting less than cordial and people all around were saying, "I can't stand that guy," etc., he would usually say something like, "maybe he's just having a bad day!" or "he's always like that...," and always with a smile on his face, without judgment. Not an ego in sight with this cat, and never a bad word about anyone or anything at any time.

Remembering sharing stories, about EAST LOS and L.A. between meals with Nolan and Patrice will ALWAYS bring a huge smile to my face. He will be sorely missed in this world, and I look forward to seeing him again in the next. THANK YOU NOLAN and PATRICE for sharing your most precious commodity - your time, kindness, stories, and generosity. ABRAZOS, VIVA LA VIDA, VAYA CON DIOS.

MONIQUE LAZARUS:
Honoring my friend and colleague Nolan Frederick Porter, who we lost last night. Such a talented yet humble gentleman. We had many great talks over the years. My heart goes out to the love of his life, his wife Patrice Zappa-Porter. You will be missed, Nolan, but in

our hearts you will "keep on keeping on."

MEGAN MEEHAN:
I couldn't find the words, so I'm sharing my husband's post. Such a wonderful man was Nolan Frederick Porter. I will miss his light. Until we meet again, my friend.

HOD MEEHAN:
This dear, sweet man…my brother in music, a master among mentors, my soulful and true friend Nolan Frederick Porter has left us for greater things. May God keep and hold him and his family. May his music lift our hearts with joy and may all who were so fortunate to be here on this path with him find peace. In love and light, rest my brother. You will be so missed and my heart aches, but you will always be found in music.

TONY MARTIN BLANK:
It is a great loss we're all feeling that Mr. Porter is not here in person, but he is still here with his songs and music and all the beautiful things that he's done in his life. I was sharing with my wife the little story that I had when I was about seven or eight that I was able to meet Mr. Porter. I love this music so much, and I do remember buying a 45 of his that I used to play at my father's restaurant. His music touched me and helped me through a lot of things. God bless you - respect and love.

JON BIGGS:
It was an honor and privilege to know you. I am very blessed to have made music with you too. Thank you, Sir! You left a HUGE impression on this planet and touched so many with your beautiful soul! Sending love and prayers to his family and amazing wife Patrice Zappa-Porter. RIP Nolan.

RICK KENDRICK:
I've got a great story to go with this picture! In Portland, Oregon, Sabi and I were to take Nolan and Monty (Neysmith) to breakfast as Pan had stuff to take care of for the show. We sat and gladly listened to their stories! When we left and I was paying up, the waiter came to me and asked if those two gentlemen I was with were famous or somebody they should know. Ha ha! I laughed and said "In certain circles, yes, very much so"! You have no idea.

From left to right: Sabina Bukovec-Kendrick, Nolan, Monty Neysmith, Rick Kendrick.

Nolan performed with Rick Kendrick's group The Inciters during a Memorial Day weekender called "Pressure n Slide" on May 26, 2018 at The Twilight Room in Portland, Oregon. Nolan and The Inciters also played at The Crêpe Place in Santa Cruz, California on April 27, 2019.

AGUSTÍ ROCAMORA DURÁ:
RIP my dear friend, Nolan Frederick Porter. For me, it was an honor to know you and above all, the way you treated me, from you to me, from equal to equal. You proved to be a real gentleman. You've left me broken. At the same time, I am very proud to have treated you, touched, spoken, hugged. If heaven exists in which you firmly believed, allow me to speak of you. You have gained a place of privilege in it. I will always keep you in my heart.

JARED ROSENBAUM:
Nolan Porter IS one of the most beautiful people to have lived - among many other traits, a lovely blend of kindness and coolness. Always fully engaged, he seemed to care so genuinely about others - their trials and successes large and small. And boy, did he love music - a man who embodied his sound and style through and through. He was a true professional with the mic, including behind the scenes at rehearsal. Everyone has shared beautiful memories of Nolan and how he touched their lives. To me, above all, he was a role model in how to let music flow through your body, a role model in true professionalism, and a role model in how to treat others, especially in how he treated Patrice Zappa-Porter - also one of my favorite people to have spent time with! The amount of respect he exhibited toward others was the gold standard, and it was made stronger by the amount of respect he had for himself. My life is truly better to have known him. He showed me how to be a better man. Thank you, Nolan. Rest easy, my friend.

ALESSANDRA IZZO:
Patrice Zappa-Porter and Nolan Frederick Porter, you are in our heart forever! RIP dear Nolan, a great person and friend as well. Patrice, we are here for you, now and forever! I will never forget our time at dinner to historical Canter's Deli in L.A.!

FRANK CLEVERLEY (photographer for page 25 top photo):

At right: Frank Cleverley with Nolan in 2010.

ARMIN BECK:
I live with my family at the Dutch/German border, and in 2015 we had the dream to do a once in a lifetime holiday. We spent four weeks with our kids in America, the country with "the endless possibilities," as we say in Germany. We already planned this trip before I did my first visit to the Zappanale in 2015. That was where I was infected by the Zappanale virus. With my lifelong friend Markus, also a Zappa fan, we decided to go to the Zappanale festival in Bad Doberan, Germany. We also went to the festival in 2016.

We had a very good time seeing and hearing the music we loved so much, while making contact with other Zappa manics and drinking plenty of "yellow water." One of the highlights of the 2016 festival was Patrice "Candy" Zappa and her husband Nolan Porter. Candy was performing with The Muffin Men. I was not previously aware of the talents of both Candy and Nolan. And then there was this great concert with superb performances from both of them. Nolan even performed a song from his own back catalog: "If I Could Only Be Sure." It was the first time I heard Nolan's lovely voice.

After their gig, there was the usual Q&A in the VIP tent, and I had a nice chat with Nolan and Candy. I told her that I would be traveling with my family to the US in about a month, and that we would be visiting L.A. And, Patrice said, "Why don't you come along for a coffee visit?"...Huh??? Did I understand her correctly??? She confirmed it and gave me her contact information. Wow!!! How nice was that?!? Fantastic!

We finally got a message from Patrice to meet in a restaurant in Van Nuys on the very last evening of our four-week holiday. Exhausted from a long trip, we struggled through the traffic in L.A. because I first had to fulfill my daughter's wish to pay a visit to the soda pop stop in L.A.'s Highland Park. Right after that, we headed to Van Nuys and found the address. Coincidentally, we parked our funny painted small escape campervan beside a white car. Suddenly, Patrice and Nolan stepped out. After a short welcome, we sat at a table in a nearly empty restaurant and chatted about...nearly everything. While my wife and three kids had more contact with Patrice, I sat towards Nolan and we talked loads about music. He asked me about my musical endeavors. I told him about several of my efforts in different musical settings, but I was honestly always in the position of being a hobby musician besides my daytime job. That is when I got to know more about Nolan's long career as a soul singer. He told me that he and Patrice got together through their passion for music and singing. Nolan also shared his view of the music industry and the inherent ups and downs that you experience as a professional musician.

I learned that both Nolan and Patrice actually had to work hard for their income and that they surely don't live a luxurious life of a soul star and sister of a rock genius. Both were very down to earth, friendly and open, and also interested in us. After we ended up having a lovely chat for about three hours of funny and serious issues, Nolan and Patrice insisted on inviting us and took over the bill. My wife took this photo with Nolan, Patrice and me at the end of this nice evening, and afterwards we headed back to a cheap motel in Inglewood near the LAX airport, where we started our west coast trip several weeks before. I went to bed both excited and exhausted, but very happy that this meeting took place. They were just lovely people!! I am very sad that such a wonderful man has left this earth. Music brings people together…or as Patrice's brother once quoted, "Music is the best!"

NEIL JONES (STONE FOUNDATION) (photos on pages 26-32):
I wanted to write a fitting tribute to my dear friend Nolan Frederick Porter. Today, the world lost a kind and decent man, whose music made us feel better about the world we live in and whose spirit cast a warm and magical glow on everyone who had the good fortune to know or meet him. His songs became anthems to so many people around the world, and his two seminal records "Nolan – No Apologies" and "Nolan" became staples in every self-respecting music fan's vinyl collection. Even though he was deeply hurt, battered and bruised by the music industry, he still never lost his desire to perform and record new music.

He was one of our first ever Stone Foundation collaborators. He taught us so much and was a soul brother in every sense of the word, recording "Tracing Paper," "Right Track," "Crazy Love," "Fe-Fi-Fo- Fum" and his own brand of enchanting and ethereal backing vocals on our much loved song "Beverley." It led to further productive years together in the shape of BBC sessions, a documentary "Keep On Keepin' On" put together by our friend Lee Cogswell, countless gigs, tours and a Nolan Porter & Stone Foundation "Live At The 100 Club" record, something I know he was deeply proud of.

He was our brother, one of the band, and thought it was as important to take music forward and record new material just as much as it was to pay homage to his joyous past. All this from a man who used to regale me about recording records with guys from The Mothers Of Invention and Little Feat, performing in L.A. with Rick James, Johnny "Guitar" Watson and Lowell George, and coming full circle and falling for the love of his life, Patrice Zappa. The man with the funky Afro that never lost that beautiful L.A. sunshine smile and penchant for peace, love, and unity.

Nolan, when your loving wife Patrice sent me a message a few weeks back asking me to contribute to a book she was curating on your life, I thought it would be the perfect opportunity to write my piece directly to you in the form of a letter—a letter to a dear friend who helped and influenced this young musician to grow (and the young man I was then) to widen my perspective on life and the precious time we have here.

Dear Nolan…

It's Neil here. We never did finish that conversation we had last summer. Last time we spoke (or indeed I spoke to you), you were heavily sedated and coming to the end of your journey here on earth, and what a journey it was, brother.

Our first introduction was when you arrived in the UK in the summer of 2010 to play a couple of special "Northern Soul" events. We were your backing band back then. When you arrived, we had done our homework on your tunes, those songs, those records. What a joy to work on them: we knew them inside out before your plane hit the tarmac, plus we were armed with a couple of songs of our own we wanted you to sing on. We'd never let you down brother, you know that by now. You gave us the first glimpses of that ever professional stage presence that you always wielded with ease. You taught me so much about interacting with an audience in those early days, taking people on an emotional journey and bringing love and light into a room.

We bonded musically, and as people almost instantly, and although a fleeting visit, it fired our imaginations to the possibilities of working more with you on new and exciting ventures. It was the start of some memorable hot summer nights at SFHQ and a chance for us to record two new Stone Foundation studio tracks with you: "Tracing Paper" and "Right Track." We knew right then we had a very special connection creatively and the same desire to move forward with fresh and exciting music. You were always a kindred spirit when it came to creating something new in the studio, and not just resting on your past successes. That said, recording with Frank Zappa's band and the basis of what would become Little Feat was a pretty high bar, and one we were always in awe of, man. Our "Nolan" and "Nolan - No Apologies" records signed, we said our brief goodbyes and looked to the future. We knew you should have more exposure when you returned, and we always knew there was our own story to be written together in the years ahead.

It always feels to me that we really met for the very first time in Los Angeles, the city of angels, down on Venice Beach in late summer of that same year. You were nursing Patrice through some health problems back then, pushing her along the boulevard in her chariot/wheelchair. I guess that was the first time I saw the true caring and compassionate guy you were. I still couldn't quite believe you and Patrice (Zappa) never knew each other when you worked with Frank's band! I loved Patrice straight away - her erudite and acerbic personality left an instant impact on me, and I could see the real love you had for each other. We bonded and made plans for the future and spoke about the million and one possibilities of a collaboration that would see us work together for years to come. A memorable day turned into a memorable evening eating Mexican food with your good friend Forrest Penner, who regaled us with stories of his recent touring duties with The Doors' Robbie Krieger and Ray Manzarek. We were that engrossed that we didn't even see Patrice leave the table and enter the side room. The next thing I remember was hearing this soulful voice booming out across the restaurant, and you turning nonchalantly to me to inform me it was Patrice next door on the karaoke. We shared a mic for the first time that night, brother, in a tiny backroom bar in a Mexican restaurant. It was the beginning of a beautiful friendship and an unforgettable adventure. Those two days with yourself, Patrice and my good friend Scott who'd journeyed along for the ride would provide the bedrock and excuse the pun... Foundation for the years to come.

Soon you'd return in 2012, and we had a plan. We'd arranged to get you some gigs on the main UK touring circuit and set off on our first bonafide tour together. The reaction to your hit songs "Keep On Keeping On" and "If I Could Only Be Sure" always blew my mind live; the love the UK crowd had for your music was one I know you deeply treasured. Throwing into the mix the new Stone Foundation tune we'd recorded together, "Tracing Paper," a tune that was very quickly becoming a crowd favorite, it felt like an unstoppable combination that could do no wrong! During that unforgettable first tour, we recorded our "Live At The 100 Club" record. The vibe and intensity that night was something I'll never ever forget. We achieved something beautiful that night, my friend. Crowd and band in perfect synchronicity, a packed out legendary venue in the heart of London, condensation dripping down the walls, oh, if we could only turn back time, man! I remember you being utterly exhausted at the end of that show, but still finding the time to sign autographs and thank everyone for spending their hard earned money to see us. Another lesson gratefully learned, my friend, and something I have continued to do to this day, no matter how spent of energy I am at the end of a performance. I remember the look on your face as we headed home that evening, the face of a man filled with pure contentment and sheer joy, the young hippie with the funky Afro that we see on your classic record sleeves was never far away when we played and toured together.

The tour rolled through the Midlands and a memorable night at The Musician in Leicester, up north and onto Blackpool, where your reaction to some of the hen dos on display had us in fits of laughter in the tour bus, especially when you read out the words "Cole's creamy clunge!" emblazoned across a gang of girls' t-shirts staggering along the roadside at 5 PM that evening! "This is a wild kinda town, uhh?" You were pretty on the money with that observation, Nolan. We ended up at our final destination of the tour, which was Guilfest in the south. It was another one of my favorites playing with you, man, especially as this was a younger crowd that probably didn't know all the material we were playing, but man, they were soon won over. My fondest memory of that day was of us listening to the headliner Brian Ferry as we left the backstage bar area with a smoke, a smile, and a warm embrace. Tired, happy and at peace with the world, I remember you saying, "It doesn't get much better than this," but we still had quite a bit more to come.

In the following year, we released a film "Keeping On Keepin' On" put together by our good friend and burgeoning young film maker Lee Cogswell. He'd followed us on our last tour documenting everything along the way. I know you would have loved to have been at the premiere in London, mate. Like I said on the phone back then, the feeling for that film was a joy to behold and is something I only looked back on last week with extreme fondness - and I'm not gonna lie - with a few tears in my eyes. It's kind of funny how time brings things into focus. The film made even more sense to me watching it some ten years on, and your words, although great at the time, seemed to carry a sledgehammer force and weight that went straight to my heart. Beautiful memories, brother, that are forever etched in the sands of time.

We also performed numerous acoustic sessions on the BBC over the years, culminating in a full band session for the BBC Craig Charles funk and soul show. I remember that session being particularly tricky at first, as we spent time getting the sound we wanted in the studio. But, as always, you were a beacon of calm and professionalism as we recorded take after take for the show. As a singer, I know that can be really tricky. The outcome was another special afternoon spent in your company, creating a little slice of musical history between our band and yourself.

In the same year we flew out to Spain to play the Euro Ye Ye festival, it was part of our tour itinerary. In the process, we were showing the "Keep On Keepin' On" film for the first time to our Spanish brothers and sisters. We played a short acoustic set at the premiere which was wonderfully well received before retiring to the hotel ahead of that night's gig. I remember distinctly the sense of disappointment we shared as 10 minutes before the gig the arena was empty, only to discover that in Spain, people like to leave it late. By the time we hit the stage, the atmosphere was electric and the crowd was at full capacity. It was another incredible moment on our journey together, more special glances across the stage and unspoken words as we hit full swing and the crowd called out for more.

Oh, to share another "Crazy Love" recording night with you, Nolan, the night we recorded that track for our "To Find The Spirit" record is still one of my favorite recording experiences ever. I know you were thinking about Patrice when you recorded those heartfelt vocals, and when I listen back to that record, it still makes my hairs stand on end. You even added some backing vocals to our "Beverley" tune. When I think of all the wonderful artists and musicians we've had inside our little musical clubhouse, no one's soul is more intwined in the fabric of that building than yours!

I miss the nights we'd spend putting the world to rights at my house or Scott's when you would stay with us in the Midlands, Nolan, and my grandfather Mick really misses them too. You guys became such great friends when you stayed with him during one of the tours we did. He always recounts the day you both visited Tamworth Castle and sneaked under the ropes to get a clearer look at the armor on display, only to be scolded like two naughty school boys by the lady guard who was very angry you both totally ignored the "Do not cross the rope" sign. He really loved meeting you and Patrice a few years back in L.A. Can you remember you guys surprised him when he was seeing my second cousins? That made his trip, man. When I ask him about you, he always says in his broad Brummy accent, "Nolan was an absolutely marvellous man."

I don't want to highlight your illness right now, or the reasons for your passing. It still feels very raw. It was your way to not burden people with your problems. I guess that's why you hid it from us so well, although I hope it serves as a sign for future generations to check out anything that troubles them! The last time we performed together was last year for our online Stone Foundation & Friends Festival, recording an acoustic version of "If I Could Only Be Sure." We've always both been a little hopeless when it comes to technology, but somehow we got there. Maybe it was the musical gods stepping in to lend a helping hand, or just the fact that we always managed to get things done in the end. Music was, and always will be, our reason for being!

These will be unforgettable memories, brother, that will only grow stronger in time, along with the music we created. I know your spirit will soar into the cosmos with all the other greats of music past, and I hope this letter reaches out into the ether and serves as a reminder to anyone reading of the great man you truly were. My heart goes out to Patrice and her extended family at this desperately sad time.

Please promise me you all raise a glass to a beautiful soul tonight, play your favorite Nolan tune, keep on keeping on towards a brighter tomorrow and cherish and remember his glorious spirit and the wonderful music and legacy he's left for us all. I can only sign off in one way, something you always told me no matter what the circumstance…"You will always be my friend in life, music and beyond."

Love you always,
Neil J xx Stone Foundation

Neil and Nolan silhouettes at Euro Ye Ye.

NOLAN PORTER DISCOGRAPHY

SINGLES (all US 7" releases unless otherwise noted):

NOLAN: Crazy Love/ What Would You Do If I Did That To You (Lizard 21003-X; May 25, 1970)

NOLAN: I Like What You Give/ Somebody's Cryin' (Live) (Lizard 45-1008; May 24, 1971)

PAUL HUMPHREY AND THE COOL AID CHEMISTS: Funky L.A./ Baby Rice (Lizard 45-1009; June 21, 1971 – Nolan is co-lead vocalist with Paul Humphrey on the A-side only)

FREDERICK II: Groovin' Out On Life/ Gwendolyn (Vulture 5002; September 13, 1971)

N.F. PORTER: Keep On Keeping On/ Don't Make Me Color My Black Face Blue (Lizard 45-1010; September 13, 1971)

NOLAN PORTER: If I Could Only Be Sure/ Work It Out In The Morning (ABC 11343; December 18, 1972)

NOLAN PORTER: Singer Man/ Oh Baby (ABC 11367; May 28, 1973)

STONE FOUNDATION FEATURING NOLAN PORTER: Tracing Paper/ STONE FOUNDATION: Dogtooth (UK Heavy Soul ROR015HS3; January 12, 2011 – Nolan is lead vocalist on the A-side only)

NOLAN PORTER AND STONE FOUNDATION: Fe-Fi-Fo-Fum/ STONE FOUNDATION: Warning Signs (UK Heavy Soul ROR044HS31; February 18, 2013 – Nolan is lead vocalist on the A-side only)

N.F. PORTER: Keep On Keeping On/ If I Could Only Be Sure (Dutch ABC/Universal 00602547222848; April 18, 2015 – Record Store Day issue limited to 1,000 copies)

STONE FOUNDATION FEATURING NOLAN PORTER: Beverley/ STONE FOUNDATION FEATURING FOUR PERFECTIONS: Pushing Your Love (UK Light Of Love Wax Co. LOLWC002; January 29, 2016 – Nolan is backing vocalist on the A-side only)

NOLAN PORTER: If I Could Only Be Sure/ Keep On Keeping On (UK Light Of Love Wax Co. LOLWC004; April 29, 2016)

NOLAN PORTER: Go-Go-Go/ Go-Go-Go (Instrumental) (Soulside Productions A/B-69-4; December 15, 2017 – Nolan is lead vocalist on the A-side only)

NOLAN PORTER: Keep On Keeping On/ If I Could Only Be Sure (UK Outta Sight OSV179; June 15, 2018)

Many similar single releases have been released in other countries.

ALBUMS (all US releases unless otherwise noted):

NOLAN: Nolan – No Apologies (LP) (Lizard A 20102; June 22, 1970)
TRACKS: Iron Out The Rough Spots; Let's Burn Down The Cornfield; What Would You Do If I Did That To You; Gwendolyn; The Fifth One/ Travelin' Song; Somebody's Gone (Mix #1); Don't Make Me Color My Black Face Blue; Fe-Fi-Fo-Fum; Somebody's Cryin'

PAUL HUMPHREY AND THE COOL AID CHEMISTS: Paul Humphrey And The Cool Aid Chemists (LP) (Lizard A 20106; April 12, 1971)
TRACKS: Funky L.A. (Nolan wrote the song and sang lead vocals with Paul Humphrey)

NOLAN PORTER: Nolan (LP) (ABC ABCX-766; January 22, 1973)
TRACKS: I Like What You Give; Groovin' (Out On Life); Somebody's Gone (Mix #2); Work It Out In The Morning; Oh Baby;/ If I Could Only Be Sure; Crazy Love; Singer Man; Let's Burn Down The Cornfield; Keep On Keeping On

BRIAN HUDSON AND THE POPULAR FRONT: Condoleezza Condoleezza (CD) (Inside Out 49512-2; August 17, 2004)
TRACKS: Sure; My Oil Man; Condoleezza; Line Of Fire; Lullaby; Minnie And Mickey; Endrun's Run; Rumination (these tracks feature Nolan Porter and Candy Zappa)

NEONFIRE: Neonfire (CD) (Crossfire Publications 9501-2; October 9, 2005
TRACKS: Alive (co-lead vocals with Candy Zappa); Lying Down (lead vocals); Hot As The Sun (backing vocals)

STONE FOUNDATION: Away From The Grain (CD) (UK The Turning Point TPCD004; October 26, 2010)
TRACKS: Tracing Paper (co-lead vocal with Neil Jones); Right Track (co-lead vocal with Neil Jones)

PATRICE "CANDY" ZAPPA: ...To Be Perfectly Frank... (digital download) (Crossfire Publications 9968-2-7; July 27, 2011)
TRACKS: Alive (by Neonfire); Hot As The Sun (by Neonfire)

NOLAN PORTER: Nolan – No Apologies (digital download) (Porterville 9969-2-6; July 29, 2011)
TRACKS: same as 1970 LP plus: Funky L.A. (Mono Single Mix; with Paul Humphrey And The Cool Aid Chemists); Crazy Love (Mono Single Mix); What Would You Do If I Did That To You (Mono Single Mix); Groovin' (Out On Life) (Mono Single Mix); Gwendolyn (Mono Single Mix); I Like What You Give (Mono Single Mix); Somebody's Cryin' (Live) (Mono Single Mix); Keep On Keeping On (Mono Single Mix); Don't Make Me Color My Black Face Blue (Mono Single Mix); Funky L.A. (Stereo LP Mix; with Paul Humphrey And The Cool Aid Chemists); Street Scene; Lying Down (Radio Edit; by Neonfire); Alive (by Neonfire)

NOLAN PORTER: Nolan (digital download) (Porterville 9970-2-2; July 29, 2011)
TRACKS: same as 1973 LP plus: If I Could Only Be Sure (Stereo Single Mix); Bird Without A Song (1978 Version); Only A Thought Away; It's Alright To Dream; City Lights; Cloudy;

What A Fool Believes; Every Little Move; I Like What You Give (1980 Version); Oh Baby (1980 version); Bird Without A Song (1980 Version); I Put A Spell On You (from the film "The Quickie"); Lying Down (by Neonfire); Alive (AAA Mix; by Neonfire)

STONE FOUNDATION: The Three Shades Of...Stone Foundation (CD) (UK The Turning Point TPCD005; September 26, 2011)
TRACKS: Tracing Paper (co-lead vocal with Neil Jones); Right Track (co-lead vocal with Neil Jones)

NOLAN PORTER & STONE FOUNDATION: Live At The 100 Club (CD; 500 copies) (UK The Turning Point TPCD006; August 24, 2012)
TRACKS: Oh Baby; I Like What You Give; Somebody (Somewhere) Needs You; Tracing Paper; Crazy Love; Fe-Fi-Fo-Fum; Gimme Little Sign; Keep On Keeping On; If I Could Only Be Sure (all tracks recorded at The 100 Club in London on July 7, 2012)

STONE FOUNDATION: To Find The Spirit (CD) (UK The Turning Point TPCD007; March 10, 2014)
TRACKS: Crazy Love (lead vocals); Bring Back The Happiness (backing vocals)

STONE FOUNDATION: To Find The Spirit (LP + CD-R) (UK The Turning Point TPLP007/(no # on bonus disc); March 10, 2014)
TRACKS: Crazy Love (lead vocals); Bring Back The Happiness (backing vocals)

NOLAN PORTER: Nolan – No Apologies/ Nolan (CD) (Porterville 9520-2; December 2, 2014)
TRACKS: same as the original LPs, except that "Burn Down The Cornfield (Remix)" replaces the mix on the second album, "I Like What You Give" is an unedited remix, and the package includes the bonus tracks "Only A Thought Away," "Bird Without A Song (1980 Version)," and "Alive (AAA Mix)" (by Neonfire)

STONE FOUNDATION: A Life Unlimited (CD) (UK The Turning Point TPCD008; August 7, 2015)
TRACKS: Beverley

STONE FOUNDATION: A Life Unlimited (clear vinyl LP + CD) (UK The Turning Point TPLP008X/TPCD008; August 7, 2015)
TRACKS: Beverley

STONE FOUNDATION: A Life Unlimited (CD + CD-R) (UK The Turning Point TPCD008/(no # on bonus disc); August 7, 2015)
TRACKS: Beverley

Nolan Porter has been on many various artist compilations. Since he was not paid for any of them, they will not be listed or promoted here!

NOLAN PORTER SESSIONOGRAPHY FOR THE LIZARD, VULTURE AND ABC LABELS (lead vocals on all tracks):

February 13, 1969: demo session at American Recorders, Studio City, California with Gabriel Mekler (production), Richard Podolor (engineer), Jerry McCrohan (drums), John Goadsby (keyboards)
TRACKS: The Fifth One (demo - tape lost); Don't Make Me Color My Black Face Blue (demo - tape lost)

March 11, 1970: Wally Heider Recording (Studio 3), Hollywood, California with Gabriel Mekler (keyboards, production), Wally Heider (engineer), Jimmy Carl Black (drums), Roy Estrada (bass) and Lowell George (guitar), Tony Elisalda (horns, conga), Clydie King (backing vocals), Venetta Fields (backing vocals), Sherlie Matthews (backing vocals)
TRACKS: The Fifth One; Don't Make Me Color My Black Face Blue

March 12, 1970: Wally Heider Recording (Studio 3), Hollywood, California with Gabriel Mekler (keyboards, production), Wally Heider (engineer), Jimmy Carl Black (drums), Roy Estrada (bass) and Lowell George (guitar), Tony Elisalda (horns, conga), Clydie King (backing vocals), Venetta Fields (backing vocals), Sherlie Matthews (backing vocals)
TRACKS: Crazy Love; What Would You Do If I Did That To You

March 13, 1970: Wally Heider Recording (Studio 3), Hollywood, California with Gabriel Mekler (keyboards, production), Wally Heider (engineer), Jimmy Carl Black (drums), Roy Estrada (bass), Lowell George (guitar), Tony Elisalda (horns, conga), Clydie King (backing vocals), Venetta Fields (backing vocals), Sherlie Matthews (backing vocals)
TRACKS: Gwendolyn; Fe-Fi-Fo-Fum

March 29, 1970: Wally Heider Recording (Studio 3), Hollywood, California with Gabriel Mekler (production), Wally Heider (engineer), Lowell George (guitar), Roy Estrada (bass), Richard Hayward (drums), William Payne (keyboards), Tony Elisalda (horns, conga), Clydie King (backing vocals), Venetta Fields (backing vocals), Sherlie Matthews (backing vocals)
TRACKS: Travelin' Song; Let's Burn Down The Cornfield

March 30, 1970: Wally Heider Recording (Studio 3), Hollywood, California with Gabriel Mekler (production), Wally Heider (engineer), Lowell George (guitar), Roy Estrada (bass), Richard Hayward (drums), William Payne (keyboards), Tony Elisalda (horns, conga), Clydie King (backing vocals), Venetta Fields (backing vocals), Sherlie Matthews (backing vocals)
TRACKS: Iron Out The Rough Spots; Fe-Fi-Fo-Fum (conga overdubs)

March 31, 1970: Wally Heider Recording (Studio 3), Hollywood, California with Gabriel Mekler (production), Wally Heider (engineer), Lowell George (guitar), Roy Estrada (bass), Richard Hayward (drums), William Payne (keyboards), Clydie King (backing vocals), Venetta Fields (backing vocals), Sherlie Matthews (backing vocals)
TRACKS: Somebody's Gone

Early June 1970 (session sheet filed October 12, 1970): The Sound Factory West, Hollywood, California with Gabriel Mekler (production), Dave Hassinger (engineer), Val Garay (engineer),

Clarence McDonald (keyboards), Tony Elisalda (saxophone, percussion), William Allen (bass), Sanford Konikoff (drums), David T. Walker (guitar), Clydie King (backing vocals), Venetta Fields (backing vocals), Sherlie Matthews (backing vocals)
TRACKS: Somebody's Cryin' (studio version)

June 15, 1970: live at The Troubadour, Los Angeles, California with Gabriel Mekler (keyboards, production, engineer), Sanford Konikoff (drums), William Allen (bass), Tony Elisalda (horns, conga), Robert Torres (saxophone), Clydie King (backing vocals), Venetta Fields (backing vocals), Sherlie Matthews (backing vocals)
TRACKS: Somebody's Cryin' (live single version)

July 31, 1970: The Sound Factory West, Hollywood, California with Gabriel Mekler (organ, production), Dave Hassinger (engineer), Val Garay (engineer), Paul Humphrey (co-lead vocal, drums), Ernest Corallo (guitar), Nathaniel Johnson (bass), Gene Pello (percussion), David T. Walker (guitar), Clarence McDonald (keyboards), Clydie King (backing vocals), Venetta Fields (backing vocals), Sherlie Matthews (backing vocals)
TRACKS: Funky L.A. (with Paul Humphrey And The Cool Aid Chemists)

February 11, 1971: The Sound Factory West, Hollywood, California with Gabriel Mekler (production), Dave Hassinger (engineer), Val Garay (engineer), Paul H. Smith (leader, bass), Richard Flowers (drums), George Walker (guitar), Clydie King (backing vocals), Venetta Fields (backing vocals), Sherlie Matthews (backing vocals)
TRACKS: Keep On Keeping On

February 17, 1971: The Sound Factory West, Hollywood, California with Gabriel Mekler (production), Dave Hassinger (engineer), Val Garay (engineer), Lee King, Jr. (leader, rhythm guitar), Paul H. Smith (bass), Richard Flowers (guitar), George Walker (guitar)
TRACKS: Keep On Keeping On (overdubs)

Mid-February 1971: The Sound Factory West, Hollywood, California with Gabriel Mekler (organ, production), Dave Hassinger (engineer), Val Garay (engineer), Mike Deasy (guitar), Paul Humphrey (drums), Ron Johnson (bass)
TRACKS: I Like What You Give

June 17, 1971: The Sound Factory West, Hollywood, California with Gabriel Mekler (production), Dave Hassinger (engineer), Val Garay (engineer), Clarence K. McDonald (keyboards), William Allen (bass), Arthur K. Adams (guitar), Paul N. Humphrey (drums), Charles M. Owens (saxophone), Oscar Brashear (trumpet), Abigail Haness (backing vocals), Bobbie Porter (congas)
TRACKS: Groovin' (Out On Life) (single and album versions)

(Some time in the early summer of 1972, Gabriel Mekler made a deal with ABC Records, Inc. to record Nolan Porter. The following sessions are shown as for ABC and not Lizard Productions.)

August 16, 1972: The Sound Factory West, Hollywood, California with Gabriel Mekler (production), Dave Hassinger (engineer), Val Garay (engineer), Clarence McDonald (keyboards),

Charles M. Owens (saxophone), Oscar Brashear (trumpet), James B. Gordon (drums), Ray Pohlman (bass), Larry Carlton (guitar), Abigail Haness (backing vocals)
TRACKS: Oh Baby (shown with the tentative title "Baby"); Work It Out In The Morning

August 24, 1972: The Sound Factory West, Hollywood, California with Gabriel Mekler (production), Dave Hassinger (engineer), Val Garay (engineer), Ronald C. Elliott (guitar)
TRACKS: Oh Baby (shown with the tentative title "Baby Oh Baby") (guitar overdub)

Late August 1972: The Sound Factory West, Hollywood, California with Gabriel Mekler (production *+, organ *+), Dave Hassinger (engineer), Val Garay (engineer), Johnny "Guitar" Watson (lead guitar *, backing vocals *), Clarence McDonald (piano *), Paul Humphrey (drums +), James B. Gordon (drums *), Ray Pohlman (bass *), Wilton Felder (bass +), Larry Carlton (rhythm guitar *), Ken Marco (rhythm guitar +), Tony Elisalda (percussion *+)
TRACKS: If I Could Only Be Sure *; Singer Man +

April 26, 1973: The Sound Factory West, Hollywood, California with Gabriel Mekler (production), Dave Hassinger (engineer), Val Garay (engineer), Ken Marco (rhythm guitar)
TRACKS: Singer Man (Single Version) (guitar overdub)

UNRELEASED TRACKS:

Nolan Porter does not have any existing unreleased tracks from the early part of his career. In more recent years, Nolan recorded these tracks which have yet to be issued:

The Fifth One (with Stone Foundation)
Slap Back (with Forrest Penner)
Cage Within
Miss My Mind

VIDEOS (all US releases unless otherwise noted):

The Quickie (DVD) (Monarch Video 7627; February 25, 2003)
TRACKS: I Put A Spell On You

Stone Foundation – Finding The Spirit (DVD) (UK self-release with no label or #; July 21, 2014)
TRACKS: Nolan Porter appears during Lee Cogswell's original film segment "Keep On Keepin' On" that was originally released in the UK on June 22, 2013

BBC MUSIC SESSIONS WITH STONE FOUNDATION:

Tracing Paper; If I Could Only Be Sure (acoustic versions with Stone Foundation's Neil Jones) - first aired August 3, 2014 on BBC Birmingham
If I Could Only Be Sure; Keep On Keeping On; Fe-Fi-Fo-Fum; Tracing Paper – first aired August 9, 2014 on "The Craig Charles Funk And Soul Show" on BBC Radio 6 Music

TELEVISION - CAREER HIGHLIGHTS:

"**American Bandstand**" – June 5, 1971 initial air date: Funky L.A. (with Paul Humphrey And His Cool Aid Chemists)
"**Soul Train**" – January 15, 1972 initial air date: Crazy Love; Keep On Keeping On

Also available from Crossfire Publications:

NEONFIRE: "Neonfire" (digital release)
PATRICE "CANDY" ZAPPA: "...To Be Perfectly Frank..." (digital release)
FRANCIS ZAPPA: "Chances: And How To Take Them"
GREG RUSSO: "Ancient Armaments: The Frank Zappa Singles Project"
GREG RUSSO: "Cosmik Debris: The Collected History And Improvisations Of Frank Zappa"
PATRICE "CANDY" ZAPPA: "My Brother Was A Mother: Take 4" (The Zappa Family Album)

COSMIK DEBRIS:

The Collected History and Improvisations

of

FRANK ZAPPA

GREG RUSSO

To subscribe to the Nolan Porter mailing list with access to exclusive recordings, please send your email to crossfirepublications@gmail.com.

www.ingramcontent.com/pod-product-compliance
Lightning Source LLC
Chambersburg PA
CBHW060424010526

44118CB00017B/2352